Praise for
Next-Level Teaching

When it comes to life, teaching, and education, Jonathan Alsheimer is a force of nature. He has the heart of a lion! *Next-Level Teaching* will inspire, motivate, and take you beyond wherever you thought you could go as a teacher!

Hamish Brewer, Principal, author of *Relentless*

The world of education needs leaders like Jonathan Alsheimer, a savvy teacher who's hungry and determined to attack the norms of the classroom experience and take education to the next level.

Paul Felder, UFC fighter, sports analyst

Kids need to believe in their dreams and have people in their lives that truly believe in them. Mr. Alsheimer shows just how powerful a teacher's influence can be in providing encouragement to go to the next level and attack life, never giving up, and accomplishing something great!

Marvin Clark II, Professional basketball player, former student

Many of us, on our journeys through life, are able to look back and identify a particular mentor or teacher who entered our adolescent lives, told us we mattered, and gave us the courage to follow our deepest desires. Jonathan Alsheimer is one such teacher, changing lives and changing cultures for his fortunate students.

John Posey, Actor, screenwriter, playwright, producer

Jonathan Alsheimer is leading a revolution of thought and practice that every school needs to join!

Matthew Schaffer, Teacher

Next-Level Teaching is raw and tactical. Jonathan's passion for authentically connecting to students and empowering teachers is inspiring. This book is going to change classrooms around the world!

Mike Smith, Author, social entrepreneur, misfit, adventurer

Jonathan Alsheimer's passion for teaching and unorthodox methods of reaching students is the real deal. As an educator for over ten years in at-risk schools, he knows what it takes to change a school's culture. His all-in approach has helped students, educators, and administrators across the country rediscover their why and their own passion. His next-level mentality has inspired many educators to think outside the box, to add little twists to a bland lesson to make it fun and engaging, and to do whatever it takes to be *that* teacher for their students. Jonathan is an inspiration to so many educators, but especially me.

Jordan Fisher, Health and physical education teacher

Jonathan challenges us to do more, seek more, and be more! Not just for the benefit of student learning but for our own personal and professional growth as educators. With friendly reminders about the importance of our roles as teachers, he nails the narrative that relationships are a crucial part of building a wicked school culture. You either crush it or you don't. It really is that simple!

Brian Aspinall, Educator, speaker, and author

Theodore Roosevelt talked about "the man in the arena." That is Jonathan Alsheimer. He writes with a credibility that can only come from someone who is walking the walk, day in and day out. *Next-Level Teaching* is not just his journey as a teacher; it is a call for every educator to realize their awesome potential and seize every moment.

Danny Steele, Educator, author, and speaker

When I read this book, I could not only feel the passion Jonathan has for seeing his students become successful but his energy to see the same for his peers and the education profession as a whole. His focus on building a classroom community where students feel their purpose is inspiring. This book is like a pep talk to get you excited for all the possibilities we can create together for students in our schools.

George Couros, Educator, author, and speaker

Next-Level Teaching gives you a window into what motivates Jonathan and how this motivation impacts teaching and student learning. Learn how to be more innovative, creative, collaborative, and how to make the choice every day to be positive for students in your school. Jonathan's experiences will inspire you to never accept that average is good enough, to think differently about what you do, and to go all in for students and your school. Be the person that makes a difference in the life of a child. Choose to be a culture builder for your class, school, and division. *Next-Level Teaching* is a must-read book.

Evan Robb, Coauthor of *TeamMakers*

Next-Level Teaching is a passionate, energetic, and engaging rallying cry to become better educators and people. By sharing personal narratives, examples, and his own dreams and ambitions, Jonathan weaves together a beautifully written book about the importance of taking risks and of making schools better for the students who need them. This book serves as a reminder to all school communities of the importance of everyone's role in building positive school culture.

Roman Nowak, Teacher, student success leader, agent of transformation,
École secondaire catholique L'Escale, Rockland, Ontario

As a parent of kids with developmental delays, I know how much of a struggle school can be for students and their families. Jonathan Alsheimer's approach to education empowers teachers to transform those everyday struggles of education into an extraordinary and engaging journey.

Jeremy Porter, Father of three

Jonathan Alsheimer understands that to be effective as an educator, we must put the student as human being first, and their brains will follow. His three questions for lesson design—find them in chapter 4—are brilliant in their simplicity, and it's no coincidence he's as successful as he is. You'll find the best of the teaching profession in this book.

Stephen Parker Zielinski, Superintendent, South Seneca Central School District

Jonathan Alsheimer pours out his fire for students and pushing boundaries in every word of *Next-Level Teaching*. As he shares his story, readers will be moved to push and go "next level" themselves to shift their school's culture and go beyond for their students.

Eli Casaus, Lead learner, principal, edu innovator

A book written from the heart by a truly inspiring educator who is not afraid to get things done a little different. This is your blueprint to becoming a next-level teacher.

Thomas Annunziata, Athletic director, teacher

If you want to be part of something special—something bigger than yourself—then you absolutely must read this book! Jonathan will inspire you and encourage you through incredible anecdotes from his classroom. *Next-Level Teaching* is sure to inspire an educational movement that you will want to join!

Alicia Ray, Educator, lifelong learner, author of *Educational Eye Exam*

Whether you are looking to increase student engagement, improve pedagogy, or simply find new strategies to implement in your classroom, this book is full of tips, ideas, and motivation that will completely revolutionize your classroom. Jonathan's passion and enthusiasm can be felt in every word of *Next-Level Teaching*!

Dr. Phil Campbell, Author, Jostens Renaissance ambassador

Get ready to take your teaching to the next level and influence the trajectory of your students with *Next-Level Teaching* by Jonathan Alsheimer! Every learner deserves teachers who are eager to take teaching to the next level and create life-changing opportunities for them. Alsheimer pours his heart into this book, sharing his experiences and getting real by breaking down how to really reach kids and transform lives.

Elisabeth Bostwick, Instructional coach, award-winning educator,
author of *Take the L.E.A.P.: Ignite a Culture of Innovation* and
Coauthor of *Education Write Now: Top Strategies for Improving Relationships and Culture*

An inspirational and energetic game changer, Jonathan's dynamic approach to creating excitement, confidence, extreme effort, relationships, influence, engagement, and success in schools is captivating and contagious. Direct strategies and examples of innovative practice make the task of creating a positive school culture straightforward. Schools and communities will benefit from the wave of next-level teachers this book will inspire.

Rosaleesh Kingi, Deputy principal, Oxley Park Public School, Sydney, Australia

From the opening paragraph of *Next-Level Teaching*, you can feel author Jonathan Alsheimer's passion and "no limits" attitude jumping out from the pages. If you are looking to rekindle your passion for teaching, then I encourage you to start reading today!

Jimmy Casas, Educator, author, speaker, leadership coach

Everyone wants to feel like they are part of something special—to belong. Jonathan Alsheimer cuts to the core of what many people miss in education. Building relationships matters! Being creative and meeting your students where they are matter! Taking what you do every day to the next level matters!

Dr. Darrin M. Peppard, Superintendent, West Grand School District, Colorado

In *Next-Level Teaching*, Jonathan Alsheimer shares his passion for teaching, his students, and life itself. Whether you are in your first year of teaching or your thirtieth, you will be motivated to move your classroom and your school in the right direction by working harder, doing your best each and every day, and inspiring others to do the same after reading this book.

Jay Billy, Principal, Ben Franklin Elementary School, Lawrenceville, NJ,
author of *Lead with Culture: What Really Matters in Our Schools*

Next-Level Teaching is the inspiration and motivation that every teacher needs. As Jake asks, "Why not die with great memories, not dreams?"

Benjamin Plummer, Teacher

Next Level
TEACHING

Next Level
TEACHING

Empowering Students & Transforming School Culture

JONATHAN W. ALSHEIMER

Next-Level Teaching: Empowering Students and Transforming School Culture

© 2020 Jonathan W. Alsheimer

All rights reserved. No part of this publication may be reproduced in any form or by any electronic or mechanical means, including information storage and retrieval systems, without permission in writing by the publisher, except by a reviewer who may quote brief passages in a review. For information regarding permission, contact the publisher at books@daveburgessconsulting.com.

This book is available at special discounts when purchased in quantity for use as premiums, promotions, fund raisers, or educational purposes. For inquiries and details, contact the publisher at books@daveburgessconsulting.com.

Published by Dave Burgess Consulting, Inc.
San Diego, CA
DaveBurgessConsulting.com

Library of Congress Control Number: 2019956637
Paperback ISBN: 978-1-951600-06-8
Ebook ISBN: 978-1-951600-07-5

Cover design by Daniel Alsheimer
Interior design by Kevin Callahan/BNGO Books

I would like to dedicate
all of my work to my loving wife, Jaime Alsheimer,
and daughters, Adleigh Noelle and
Sadie Quinn. My loves, you inspire me to push further,
work harder, and be the best father and husband
I can be. I love you!

Adleigh and Sadie
Never be afraid to make your dreams a reality.
You are both my Cinderellas, and never let anyone
ever tell you that you cannot accomplish something
you've always dreamed of!

Contents

CONTENTS

Part Two
Teacher Outlook

Chapter Six

Chapter Seven

Chapter Eight

Chapter Nine

Conclusion

FOREWORD

The Heart of a Lion

Hamish Brewer

Jonathan Alsheimer ("Jake," to those who are close to him) is already hustling and working before most people have had their first cup of coffee.

One of Jonathan's passions is mixed martial arts, and when he took on the challenge of fighting in a bout, I got to witness the same incredible attitude and dedication he displayed in the classroom in the ring. (How many principals can say that about their teachers?) The words *no* and *can't* are not in Jonathan's vocabulary. He would rather die trying than not try at all.

I also witnessed a life-defining moment for him—a moment when anyone else would have chosen to quit or opted out, and Jonathan opted in! When others would have made up excuses, he showed us all—his colleagues and his students—what it looks like to be an inspiration when the chips are down. He took a failure and turned it into a lesson, showing yet again what it means to go one more round with life, to get back up, to never quit. This is Jonathan's heart and soul, and it's on full display in *Next-Level Teaching*.

He doesn't let *anything* get in the way of making a difference.

Jonathan's character in the classroom is no different than it is outside of it. He is hungry for success and passionate about helping others—he's as devoted to his students as he is loyal to his friends and family. He gives no quarter and doesn't take a backstep for anything when he's doing what's best for his students, his friends, or his family. There is nothing he wouldn't do for them. As an educator, Jonathan is fierce. As a person, he is larger than life.

I know that he truly believes that there is nothing he can't pull off when it comes to inspiring and uplifting his students and school. He does not limit himself to an ordinary mind-set. It's not unusual for Jonathan to dream big when planning an opportunity for his students or school, and he is relentless about getting what he wants for his students and school. The kind of thinking he shares with us in *Next-Level Teaching* has led to opportunities for students to meet with UFC fighters and MTV stars and incredible contributions to the school from apparel companies.

I've seen his unwavering love for his students and his implacable belief that we should help them become all that they can be. Teachers talk all the time about the opportunity we have to make a difference and to disrupt the norm; Jonathan grabs those opportunities. He doesn't let anything get in the way of making a difference for his students, and his example shows that we should do the same for our schools.

We as educators have the opportunity to engage our students, to create lively classroom and school environments, and ultimately to build, cultivate, and maintain powerful relationships with our students. In *Next-Level Teaching*, Jonathan shows us what can be accomplished when teachers truly believe in every single student. He teaches us how to turn around a student's day, how to inspire students to engage in academics, and most importantly how to win at life.

Next-Level Teaching is real, authentic, and relevant. It is a reflection of the conversations and interactions that Jonathan has on a daily basis with his students and colleagues. It shows us that nothing in life is given; it's earned through hard work, dedication, and effort. It shows us what it means to be who we say we are when no one's looking, to do what we said we would do, to be the example for those needing one, and to stand tall for what is right and good in life.

Be prepared to be inspired and challenged by *Next-Level Teaching*, to elevate yourself both professionally and personally, to look in the mirror and be able to say that you're better for your colleagues, family, and students. It's your time right now. Go out with the heart of a lion, seize your moment, and don't look back.

This book oozes intensity, passion, and power like no other book for teachers, and by writing it, Jonathan has created an opportunity for us all to take our teaching to the next level.

Thank you, Jake, for sharing this with the world and inspiring us all to greater heights.

Chapter One

Take It to the Next Level: Why Not?

As I sat in the back of the plane going hundreds of miles an hour, with almost zero training, I was surprised at how calm I could remain on the outside. I'd thought for sure that I would be freaking out—I was about to do something that could kill me, after all.

My brother Jordan was the first of about ten jumpers that day. When the door of the plane opened, he looked back with a grin that reached ear to ear. All I could think was how jealous I was that he was going first. Next thing I knew, he leaned out of the plane, and he was gone. Watching him disappear into the sky only tripled the excitement that was building inside me.

That wasn't true for the other jumpers on the plane. One by one I saw them try to mask their nervousness with nonstop chattering, fidgeting hands, and bouncing feet, all trying to hide the fact that they didn't want to take the big leap they had signed up for. They were really scared of the possibility of falling thousands of feet. One would-be jumper had even refused to board the plane before takeoff, realizing at the last minute that he was afraid to fall to his doom.

I understood. I mean, there was a reason that they'd made us sign waiver after waiver in the case of possible injury—or death.

Finally, it was my turn. I peeked out of the plane as I sat with my feet dangling into the sky for what seemed like a full minute. My heart was pounding, and I could feel the surge of adrenaline. I had been instructed to exit the plane in a very specific way: with my head tilted up, my back arched, and my pack straps held tight with both hands. Getting anything wrong could lead to a bad fall or even a nasty collision with the plane before my initial descent got started.

I felt two taps on my shoulder. That was the cue. I leaned forward and we were falling!

Once I was in the sky with my tandem instructor, I was in the fastest free fall I could ever have dreamed of. If you have never gone skydiving, I'm telling you it's a must! The feelings of fear and excitement are something you have to experience for yourself. As exhilarating as plummeting through the sky was, once my parachute opened the thrill was over, and it was pure bliss. I could see for miles and miles, and it was beautiful.

Your influence can stir the heart of your school and spread like wildfire.

The sad thing is that many people are too afraid to take that opportunity, so they will never experience those moments of exhilaration, wonder, and beauty. The same can be said of teaching. Too often people are comfortable with what they are used to, with what they know. Stepping outside the box and using your own unique flair to create something different can seem as scary as dangling from a plane about to jump. Thinking about what could go wrong can hold anyone back. But it is in that moment that you can either stay stagnant as an educator or propel yourself, your class, and your school to the next level by doing something as simple as leaning forward and stepping through the fear.

I think back to that would-be jumper who refused to get on the plane. Being afraid—what I think of as a *why mentality*—kept him on the ground and kept him from experiencing something truly incredible. That mentality will keep so many great people from doing amazing things. It will keep too many of us from becoming great teachers.

Sometimes, of course, we need to ask why. It's the basis of many great questions, a powerful challenge when we find something that is clearly wrong or needs to be changed. But too often in our personal lives, the word *why* can hold us back from accomplishing amazing things. It's an excuse, a chance to think up reasons why that amazing thing we're considering can't be done. Why try something new or why go after a big dream or why chase a goal? "It won't happen," some people say. "I'll just fail. It will be a waste of my time," say others. *Why* is the reason something is not going to happen. *Why* limits our possibilities and outcomes. *Why* puts our future in a box with no way out.

Instead I say: *Why not?* Why can't I do something great? Why not chase a dream? Why not die with great memories, not dreams?

I grew up playing sports, and I came to love mixed martial arts (MMA), most notably the Ultimate Fighting Championship (UFC). These guys are crazy: they fight in a cage! That was enough for me to want in. I didn't desire a whole career of fighting—that was never my interest. I loved the training. I loved the preparation for battle. I loved the discipline these professionals needed to master a craft that many saw only as barbaric. I even fought once. It was a middleweight title fight, a big deal for someone with zero fights on their record. I was up against a two-time champion with over sixteen fights, and our fight was the main event, the last and most important fight of the evening.

I lost the fight, but it was such a brawl that the commentator came up to me afterward and told me it had been the fight of the night. I should not have even had a title fight; I should not have had sponsors (I reached out to every major mixed martial arts clothing brand I knew, and companies who usually sponsored championship UFC fighters were sending me clothing and gear), but I had it all because I refused to settle for anything less. I took a risk. Whether in the cage, in the classroom, or in life, the only limitations we have are the ones we put on ourselves.

Why not look at every available avenue to motivate and inspire students? Teaching is not about facts on a page or on a whiteboard. Bringing our teaching to the next level means taking chances in the classroom, from using stories of our personal lives to trying new activities—even when you're worried they might utterly flop. It is up to us to make things happen in the classroom. Nothing happens when we are standing still. We need to embrace the adventure.

I am a middle school teacher. What business do I have working with the UFC, major clothing brands, television celebrities, professional athletes, sports agents, and movie producers? Well, I ask, why shouldn't I? Why not? I can create a classroom full of fun and adventure, one that students, years after they leave school, will remember. School can be a place that students want to be, a place that is so fun they forget they are actually learning—but they are.

With any big risk there can be a great reward or great failure. You don't have to live your life to the extreme or jump out of planes or be a martial artist. There are plenty of risks in teaching. You need to take chances to build relationships, create engaging lessons, and establish a lively classroom environment. Things might go wrong. The work can be exhausting. But the rewards are well worth it.

We are all in this together, and we all make mistakes. We need to understand that it is OK to make mistakes and to keep having fun and continuing to aspire and drive shifts in the cultures of our schools. That starts with you. You can change your school's culture from negative and depressing to positive and happy. Your energy, love of education, and your ability to create a game with one dry-erase marker on a whiteboard is enough to capture an entire room's attention. Students will race to be first in your classroom, and when the bell rings, they'll be complaining that class is over so soon. Because of the learning experiences you've created, when they do leave your classroom, your students will change the energy in the halls and their other classes. A school-wide positive culture will take hold, with teachers loving what they do and students enjoying learning.

Principals want teachers like that—they crave teachers like that. They want teachers willing to do what it takes to perfect their craft, next-level teachers that will heighten the educational experience in their classrooms and schools. You are that teacher.

The fact that you opened this book proves that you are willing to do whatever it takes. You have that X factor. You are searching for ways to improve, looking for answers to tough questions, and ready to prove that you are willing to go beyond the everyday to become a next-level teacher for your students. You, like so many teachers, are not satisfied with the unsuccessful norms in education. You are not satisfied with being an average teacher for your students. You are not satisfied with just clocking in and collecting a paycheck. Your desire, your energy, your passion is what every school needs. It is what every classroom needs. It is what all students need.

Let that energy charge your teaching. Be the teacher your administrators will talk about to everyone they meet. Inspire, motivate, and promote academics through highly engaging lessons and positive relationships. It is time for us as educators to live the saying "You can do anything you set your mind to." Be the teacher students gravitate to, and become a defining person in their lives. Your influence can stir the heart of your school and spread like wildfire. Actively and passionately influence your classroom and school's culture. That is the impact of a next-level teacher and the power of student engagement.

Chapter Two

Great Players Produce Great Teams: *Elevate the Teaching Game*

rowing up I loved sports. I had a true passion for baseball and basketball. I remember watching some of the best teams in sports history in the 1990s. Love them or hate them, I watched the Yankees roll over teams and win multiple World Series titles. I remember legendary coach Mike Krzyzewski building the Duke University men's basketball program into a powerhouse. Most vividly, I remember watching Michael Jordan—arguably the greatest basketball player of all time—his teammate Scottie Pippen, and Hall of Fame coach Phil Jackson of the Chicago Bulls as they ruled the NBA side by side. From 1991 to 1998 they won six NBA championships. Throughout my childhood I dreamed of being on a dominant team like the Bulls.

Even though over time players came and went, every player on that team had the same unwavering work ethic, and they shared a goal: to win the NBA championship title. Recalling all of those times I watched the Bulls totally dominate the court in the '90s, one thing is perfectly clear: Every single one of the teams, the Yankees, the Duke Blue Devils, and the Bulls, had great players all committed to working together. No matter how good Michael Jordan was, there was always another player doing what needed to be done at any given time in order to push the Bulls to victory.

Those players did not have to be asked; they actively looked for ways to make their team better. They sought out ways to win games and become a successful franchise. Each of those players put in the work, the practice, and the hours to perfect their craft. Players did not just show up fifteen minutes before the game, lace up their shoes, and win championships. They devoted time and effort, made sacrifices, and looked for ways to improve so the team would reach its fullest potential. They created a culture of winning. A culture that was not only positive but also one you could not help but get caught up in. Hard work and success were not only required but rewarded. Most importantly, those players did not sit back and wait for success to come to them. They created that culture, they shaped their success, and they cultivated their destiny.

The Lessons of Sports in Schools

Can you imagine a school with an environment so incredible, so electric that not only the students but even the teachers get caught up in the excitement that has been created? Can you picture a place where you never know what to expect because around every corner something fun and entertaining is waiting? If you can, you know the effect a positive school culture can have on every student and every teacher.

What is a positive school culture? It's what happens at a school that focuses on fostering relationships between students and teachers. It's easy to tell when a school has it. At a school like this, tears are an inevitability at the conclusion of the academic year because the students and staff have created such strong bonds.

This kind of school culture doesn't happen on its own, and it doesn't happen with ordinary teachers. The kind of school I'm talking about requires teachers who are willing to step outside their comfort zones and create something special, teachers who go beyond the ordinary. That's the kind of next-level teacher that you can be.

Too often teachers think our jobs are limited to what happens between the four walls of our classrooms and that our influence stops at the doors to the hallways. We think we cannot impact the school as a whole. But in fact teachers have the greatest power to influence and inspire change in schools, because we have the most personal contact with students each day. Your influence can create something amazing, if you have the right strategies to bring your classroom and your school to the next level. There are many ways to influence a school's culture, even when teachers might feel like they have no options.

To begin a movement of positive change and cultural growth in schools, teachers need to be three key things: passionate, energetic, and engaging. First, teachers have to have a burning ambition to make an impact every single day. Second, teachers need to bring energy into the building, into their classrooms, into the hallways, and everywhere they go. Finally, teachers need to engage students, not only as instructors but on a personal level, in the halls, at lunch, wherever they can make an impact. When teachers bring passion and energy to their work and make it a priority to get involved with their students, the doors of possibility are blown wide open.

Forgettable Teachers

When a school is drowning in negativity and failure, the problem is not the students, and it's not the lack of trendy academic strategies. The problem is a mind-set. It's people thinking, "I'm only a teacher. What can I do?" It's the idea that a teacher does not have the power to do anything beyond the walls of their classroom. Educators who limit themselves, who fear failure, who give up in frustration that they cannot change the status quo will be detrimental to the positive, energetic climate that every school hopes to obtain. Teachers with a lethargic attitude toward education have a negative influence on everyone around them.

Teachers have the greatest power to influence and inspire change in schools.

Most often these teachers become forgettable in all that they do. We've all had a teacher like this. We remember only the fact that they were, in fact, forgettable. They show up to work, punch in, and punch out, with no desire for anything other than their paycheck at the end of the week. These teachers are working simply to work, not working to inspire. But along the way, they create a negative atmosphere that degrades and depresses students, teachers, and administrators alike, even those just moving through the halls with whom they have no interaction. There are constant behavioral problems in and out-side of their classrooms. Because of educators with attitudes like that, teachers feel as though they work in a thankless world, students live in a punitive learning environment, and administrators struggle just to hold their heads above water.

This is the abyss schools can become, the depths of despair and hopelessness they can fall to. These schools exist; many of us have worked in them. We know far too well the feelings of frustration they engender. They make us question our purpose and whether we can make any difference at all. We get to the point where we hate our jobs. Ultimately we throw our hands up, wondering how it's possible that our school has fallen so far. But this does not have to be the end game.

No Shadows in Education

A simple shift in mind-set can be the necessary change you need to fulfill your potential as an educator. You can see just how much of an impact you can truly make just by becoming more involved in your school.

In order to successfully build a dynamic atmosphere in your school, you must be seen. Principals do not want their teachers standing off to the side, waiting for opportunities to get involved with students or the school. You have to find every chance to be a positive, noticeable influence. Leaders lead from the front, not from behind a desk! Be in the halls during transitions, engage with students and the community in after-school events, and look for additional ways to make an impact on your school. You need to move around the school and build relationships with students. Take part in as many fun activities as the school offers. Take spirit week to the next level by getting everyone you meet involved. Give no one the choice to opt out. Challenge everyone, including teachers, students, and administrators, to be part of something.

You cannot change the school's culture or the future of any student by standing off to the side idly watching. You have to go where the game is being played. Get in the mix, get the crowd fired up at sporting events, create hype at the pep rally, and start challenges and events that energize the student body.

Sometimes you might have to go out of your comfort zone to do this. You might have to be more than a teacher and take on a bigger personality than you might have outside of school. It can help to think of yourself as playing characters: cheerleader; game show host; hype man; carnival barker; whatever it takes to get as many students and teachers involved as you can.

When you make other people at your school feel important and valued, you'll see that they will become actively involved in building school culture themselves. This creates a sense of ownership for everyone within the school, a sense of pride, and a powerful positivity. It starts with you, but it will quickly snowball and become an avalanche—a movement.

You cannot wait for someone else to begin such a movement. You are the movement. So let's get the ball rolling and change the game of education together.

Get in the Game

What's the key to going from a failing, struggling school to one that's thriving? It's not some magical pedagogical method that only a few are privy to; it's not more technology or the newest educational program. The most important thing in turning around a school is a total overhaul of a negative culture, a change of atmosphere that comes from the energy that can only be created by teachers who walk the halls and interact with students every single day.

Great players produce great teams, and they use their strength to bring up the players around them and elevate the game to the next level. Teachers, too, can do this. Great teachers can produce other great teachers. You need to pull in the people around you. The power of a team in the world of education is tremendous. Working together, teachers can conquer problems others find insurmountable. Educators who form a unit can work together with a common mission, with a connection like a championship sports team that's always on the same page, calling out play after play, and executing them to perfection.

Just as the great sports teams of the 1990s worked to forge their successes, so can next-level educators drive the success of their schools. Such a formidable group can take a seemingly impossible task and produce amazing results, but more importantly, they can take a whole school to the next level by creating a dominant, positive, energetic school culture.

Principals do not need teachers with every academic strategy in their pocket. Anyone can learn new tricks in education by going to Pinterest or hitting up Google. In five years those trendy new strategies will be obsolete. Teachers with a positive attitude who are driven by passion, energetic, and ready to create change will always make schools better. Schools need teachers who will hunt down ways to be assets not only in their classroom but also throughout the school. Students need teachers who will engage with them everywhere. The actions of educators like this can be felt in other grade levels, by students and teachers, and the impact can be so strong that students in all grade levels know a teacher's name.

Sometimes the most effective way to *generate excitement* in teachers and students is to use nonacademic strategies.

Sometimes the most effective way to generate excitement in teachers and students is to use nonacademic strategies. Taking advantage of even the smallest opportunities, like getting the crowd hyped up at a basketball game or being the most vocal supporter of spirit week or challenging other classes to outdo your class in raising money for cancer research. Pull others into painting their faces, wearing school colors, and creating unique costumes at events. These are some of the many powerful ways that can change a school, raise the bar, and most importantly, get everyone involved in the process.

Getting to the Next Level

Our schools do not need more teachers complaining about what they do not have, who is at fault, who is not doing their job, or how bad the students are. What your school desperately needs, what your principal craves, and what your community is longing for is a next-level teacher, someone willing to take it upon themselves to create change. Be *that teacher.*

Students will remember because you did things that others were not willing to do. Your energy, your passion, and your ability to engage both teachers and students will inspire others to come along with you. Do the heavy lifting and don't wait for someone else to do the work. Dig in and take on all challenges. Fight back against any negativity you encounter, push back against failure, and eradicate frustration and disappointment when they threaten your school. Stand tall and ride head on into the storm, taking your school and your teaching to the next level!

Takeaways

- Teachers have the greatest potential to create change and influence their schools.
- Energize the student body through your participation in school events.
- Find every chance to be a positive role model.

Next-Level Discussion

In what ways could you make a powerful next-level influence on your students and school outside of your classroom?

PART ONE

Classroom Dynamics

Chapter Three

Classroom Branding: War Paint and Food Drives

I was marching around the room, yelling. The Scottish army—my students—had disbanded in fear at the sight of the massive English force standing ready for war across the battlefield. But like William Wallace in the movie *Braveheart*, I wasn't going to let them run. I jumped up on top of a desk, and the students looked on in shock, wondering what was about to happen next—and what it had to do with a canned-food drive.

They were excited and entertained all at once. With the class engaged, I told them that if we were going to get involved in the school's fund raiser, we had to make a statement.

"The English will have to take us seriously. I don't want partial participation, I want students who are willing to go the extra mile."

I called out Wallace's epic words from *Braveheart*: "They may take our lives, but they'll never take our freedom!"

The students roared to life.

They were no longer students sitting at their desks in Mr. Alsheimer's class. They were the newest members of Alsheimer Nation, battle ready, covered in war paint, and committed to collecting more canned goods than any other class in the school.

Creating a Classroom Identity

One of the most effective tools for creating enthusiasm and engagement in your classroom is identity or branding, which allows you to create something special for your students to be a part of. And everyone wants to be a part of something special.

> Good teachers look for ways to make change happen. *Great teachers* find the smallest opportunities and make miracles happen.

Classroom branding can increase student buy-in and promote academic success. Teachers can create new levels of engagement by creating a classroom brand, family, or team. Teachers can challenge their students to compete at something. When classrooms come together, students feel empowered by belonging to something unique, and they take ownership of their learning in incredible ways. I've seen them work harder, behave better, and forge incredible bonds because of the kinship they feel. What follows is an increase in student motivation, focus, work completion, and even assessment scores.

So how does a next-level teacher bring a classroom together in such a powerful way? Three key tools are leadership, inclusivity, and engagement. Everyone wants to be part of something bigger than themselves, and as a leader, it's the teacher's job to create that bigger thing for students. Essentially you establish a kingdom within your classroom walls. Students are looking for something special when they come to school, something different. When a teacher creates something special like a classroom with its own identity and they provide strong leadership, the development of strong student-teacher relationships follows. When I created my own classroom brand, I called it Alsheimer Nation.

Just like a nation, for a classroom brand to work, it's got to have strong leadership, but it also has to include everyone. All of the students who walk through my door are part of Alsheimer Nation. I won't allow partial buy-in or partial participation. The most important thing is that every student in the room is in the group. There is no division; it's us against the world. A classroom is strongest when everyone is working together. Simply put, classroom branding means helping students take ownership of their class by creating a family atmosphere. This kind of team bonding creates opportunities for students to build relationships in a completely unique way.

Kings aren't born in *castles.*

But even though my classroom brand is named after me, the teacher, the students have to be the ones who take ownership of it. For that to happen, they've got to be a part of creating it. Allowing students to be a part of the process increases their buy-in. When you create your brand, have your students come up with a classroom logo around its name. A logo is a key component that allows the group to identify as a single united team. In my classes, the Alsheimer Nation logo becomes a powerful icon. In Alsheimer Nation, students also create a hand signal so we can show our unity without being verbal or disruptive to another classroom around us. Another fun way to get students engaged in the brand is to have them come up with cool slogans to represent the classroom for the year. For example, students can play off the popular slogans like "Just Do It" or "Got Milk?"

When I first fully established Alsheimer Nation, my classes changed. Branding improved student engagement with the materials, which led to academic success, and it led to better classroom behavior. I realized that I had created something special, something useful, but most importantly, something powerful. And I knew I could take it to the next level.

The Insurrection Spreads

Alsheimer Nation was never more successful than the year it worked in conjunction with the school-wide canned-food drive. As soon as I heard about the drive, I knew I would use it as an opportunity to establish Alsheimer Nation with my newest group of students. That's when I did my William Wallace routine, leading my students to rally around a shared mission.

I used the school announcements about the food drive to make funny messages of my own, setting challenges for my students to collect more food than other classes in our grade level or even the whole school. As part of my branding, I often use media tools. When *The Dark Knight Rises* came out, I used iMovie to make a video and altered my voice to sound like the ominous character Bane to deliver a challenge between Alsheimer Nation and the rest of the school.

I also saw the canned-food drive as an opportunity to take branding outside of my classroom and positively impact the whole school's culture. I decided to start a school-wide competition, creating class-versus-class competitions and school-wide challenges as a way to connect and engage all students.

When the school fund raiser began, Alsheimer Nation sent out an over-the-top and in-your-face video directly challenging any and all classes to take us on. Almost immediately, the rest of the school became galvanized to form a collective to bring down Alsheimer Nation. Our mission and our excitement had spread like a wildfire into the rest of the school, and now they had their own mission.

It was the best thing that could have happened to my class. Alsheimer Nation became even stronger as a result. We also had a plan. We worked in total secrecy, and we relied on each other completely to work in unison. Other teachers took note, and they even sent students to investigate what we were doing, spying on us and asking my students for information. Fun spread throughout the school, and the canned-food drive—in our class and in every class—was a great success.

After that first challenge, the academic nature of my classroom began to change, and the students began to work together in a way I can describe only as family-like. We could joke around with one another. The students were brothers and sisters led by a common cause. We accepted all challenges and no matter the outcome, we put in our best effort.

Those teachers who saw how successful Alsheimer Nation was quickly began creating their own classroom brands that lasted well beyond the canned-food drive. They developed classroom names and logos, and they set challenges to see who could overtake the infamous Alsheimer Nation in any way. Classes across the school began forming alliances, getting involved in friendly rivalries, and eventually even challenged each other in which class could score highest on the next unit test.

As I walked down the halls, I saw logos, posters, and challenges taped to the doors of opposing classes. The students had yearned for excitement, and now they had it. There was no more of the drudgery of a monotonous school day. Classroom branding had become a tool for building enthusiasm throughout the school. This is what next-level teaching is all about: using small techniques to change the nature of your classroom and ultimately impact the culture of your entire school.

How to Build Your Nation

You, too, can create an atmosphere that supports academics and makes school a place students *want* to be with classroom identity.

This kind of branding doesn't have to be built on the back of some monumental event like a school fund raiser, and it doesn't have to happen all at once. A close-knit classroom environment can be built with everyday tasks and assignments. Homework or project completion can be the challenge. Consider starting with a simple academic competition between your period-one class and period-two class, like a challenge for the best score on a unit test.

You can always find opportunities to create your classroom brand with a competition. Many students are motivated by competition, but be sure to create a fun atmosphere around whatever you are establishing. Students will get excited about what you are excited about.

One job of the teacher is to set the tone in the classroom. It can be whatever you want it to be, but do not expect the students to jump in headfirst without your leadership. It is up to you to get them excited. You tell them the story. Discuss the plans, get students excited, require full participation, and bring the entertainment to your class. Give them a reason, and they will do the rest.

Whatever it is, the first challenge should last a few days to a week, but it must be continuous during that time period. It has to be routine. You cannot start this one day and forget it the next. The classroom branding process works best when you bring it about for the duration of a single challenge and continue it for the duration of the school year with more challenges.

Once the challenge is finished, it's crucial that you tell the students how proud you are, no matter the results. Students respond better to encouragements that center on effort rather than final results. If it's a competition, someone's bound to lose the first challenge, and they might feel discouraged. Use the outcome as an opportunity to build relationships and to have real conversations with them. If the challenge was a test, use the results in a conversation about ways to build study habits.

Once you've gotten comfortable with branding and challenges, you can take things to the next level by reaching out to other teachers to join in. Maybe you can have your entire group of classes challenge another teacher's classes in the same core subject. Other classes will want to join in on the fun. Students might seem like they don't care until you call them out, and then it is all-out war, which makes school fun for everyone.

Getting to the Next Level

Good teachers look for ways to make change happen. Great teachers find the smallest opportunities and make miracles happen.

It is the teacher's job to do something special, and when you do, the students will want to join in. The right experiences can enable students to look at school in a different light. Challenges and adventures like the ones described in this chapter can become the moments that students look back on and remember, and they can make you that one teacher they will always remember. You can be the one teacher that included them when they needed to be part of something special. You can be the one that took their education to the next level.

Takeaways

- Students will get excited about what you are excited about. Create an atmosphere where you inspire and motivate your students. Find ways to get them excited and establish the tone for the year.
- Engage students in creating a classroom brand. Include a name and logo for them to rally around and feel a sense of ownership in.
- Involve everyone. Capitalize on opportunities to create competition both within the classroom and within the whole school.

Next-Level Discussion

Great teachers strengthen classroom culture by making things exciting and different. In what ways could you implement your own classroom brand, taking your classroom to the next level and making it unique?

Chapter Four

The Power of Student Engagement: Are We Having Fun Yet?

The most engaging teacher I ever had, one of my inspirations for becoming a teacher, is also my favorite teacher: my dad. At the risk of sounding totally biased, I can say that he is a teaching legend. Everyone knew him as someone who truly cared, someone who would easily become their most beloved teacher. When students walked into his class, they knew they were going to have fun. He could get even the most unmotivated student to work for him, even the most disrespectful student to call him "sir," not out of compliance but out of respect and love.

He was unmatched in his motivation to take his classroom and school to the next level. He took his classes on trips to places like the Baseball Hall of Fame, brought soldiers who fought in WWII to speak to the class, and sent students around the school on search-and-destroy missions to teach them about the Vietnam War. He had many superpowers, but the ability to find every opportunity to make learning fun was one of his best, and it's something that all teachers should practice. Instead of a superpower, you might call it a skill: creating student engagement. Whatever you call it, it's a key element of next-level teaching.

Getting Engaged

On my educational journey I have found many teachers who give their all to their students. They put every bit of their heart and soul into classroom activities to bolster student-teacher relationships, get students engaged, create opportunities for student collaboration, and improve content retention. These teachers try to create an energetic atmosphere in which students cannot help but get pulled into the lessons. This kind of energy makes for a happy class of students. Administrators walk by these classrooms and look in because of the noise. What they see is a group of students fully immersed in learning. Every administrator and superintendent wants to see this in their schools. They want students to be smiling and laughing, but most importantly, they want students to be highly engaged in the learning process. They know that when teachers create this kind of classroom culture, students are happier and more attuned to the classroom activities on a daily basis.

Go for it and have some fun because school *should be fun!*

You can create a snowball effect within your school. Students will eventually leave your classroom. The joy and love of learning you wrap them in will influence their choices when they interact with other students and teachers in the future. Your positive classroom culture can circulate through the halls, into other classrooms, and throughout the school building. The culture you created, the lasting impression you leave on your students, has a direct influence on the rest of the school. Students can become more positive toward their peers and other teachers. Teachers will see and hear about what you are doing and follow in your footsteps. Administrators will be excited because, as studies show, increased student engagement decreases behavioral problems. Consistent and lasting student engagement in the classroom can affect the entire school.

It all starts with a teacher who walks through the school's doors bursting with inspiration and ideas, ready to take the world by storm and create something different. Students will run to that teacher's class with a smile because they know something cool is inevitable. This excitement and energy can only be created by the classroom teacher who is willing to step out of their comfort zone—the kind who always seems to have had an extra cup of coffee that morning. Teachers like this become swept up in the roles of teacher, motivator, and entertainer.

It might be an unfortunate side effect of the modern world, but even education is driven by students' need to be entertained. We must accept that and use it to our advantage. The next-level teacher willingly takes on the role of entertainer if that's what it takes to keep students engaged. The result of being an entertainer is a classroom with happy, excited, and highly motivated students.

In my classroom, emotions run high, and I want them to. That doesn't mean students are throwing themselves on the floor or yelling at each other. I encourage students to show their emotions in a constructive and controlled way, as I am a firm believer that emotion should be part of the classroom. It means students are feeling something, and emotions can establish a more positive learning environment. They provide opportunities for relationship building and personal interactions between students and teachers.

Breaking Free from Boredom

My educational philosophy on student learning, specifically related to the importance of increased student engagement, comes from this simple conclusion: if you are bored, so are your students! Teachers cannot complain about students putting their heads down during instruction, failing to be motivated to study for exams, or talking to other students in the classroom if we would do the same thing.

Here are some important questions to ask when constructing unit guides, lesson plans, and developing activities to help our students to retain content knowledge.

- Would I learn the content objective today?
- Would I be motivated?
- Would I enjoy this?

Whenever I develop a lesson plan I always ask myself these questions. If my answer to any of them is no, I scrap the idea and move on to something else. I search for ways to turn something that's boring into something that's exciting.

One great way to change an activity that is boring is through the use of games. Competition, goals, and fun breathe excitement into a task. As we saw in the discussion about classroom branding, many students gravitate toward competition, and it can increase student buy-in.

Sure, I'm passionate about teaching, but students are passionate about a lot of things, and that's not usually learning. Find out what they get excited about and use that to your advantage to make them eager to learn. Games can get even the least competitive student pulled into the group mentality: students want to be a part of what is happening. I use competition and games as much as I can, almost weekly. It drives student engagement because it creates an atmosphere of fun that enhances the student-teacher relationship and generates a more positive learning environment.

A teacher once told me, "I do not play any kinds of games in class. We do not have time for that kind of stuff." I can tell you this: there is a reason my test scores are always high and my students are more motivated now than they were ten years ago. It is not because I care only about test scores or data or focus only on instruction. It is because I adapt my teaching to reach my students. I will turn over every rock and use any strategy, academic or nonacademic. If it reaches my students or increases motivation, or improves academic results, I am going to do it. You make your game plan fit your players; you do not make your players fit your game plan!

When you do something—like playing a game—that seems to have nothing to do with the curriculum, it can engage your students by incentivizing them.

Bringing doughnuts into class, making root beer floats with students, or telling them a personal story (that relates to the content) can all be incentives. Strategies that are nonacademic can produce some amazing academic results.

By creating a classroom culture that is unique, you show them a new path in education. Do what you need to get the best results. Do things differently, and your students will remember you. As a teacher who has been able to get my classes to achieve at the highest levels, I say go for it, and have some fun.

Turning Games into a Game Plan

Games are a prime way I use fun to increase engagement in my classes. Recently, my students needed to learn to recognize the location of each country involved in WWI on a map for a test. That's a lot of countries, some of whose names are hard to pronounce and remember, and locating them on a blank world map is no easy task. Still, I told my students that I guaranteed they would ace any map quiz on WWI. One of my students said, "Sorry, Mr. A, but I can't even read these, so I'm not passing."

Little did he know what was about to happen. First, I did what many teachers would, I handed out blank maps and had the students color and label the countries they needed to learn. Once that was done, I gave students a time limit and had them study their maps first individually at the start of class each day for a few days and in groups at the end of class.

Then we played map wars.

I divided the students into teams, and one at a time a student from each team would come to the front of the room. We played student versus student and table versus table, and everyone got pulled into the fun.

This is just one example, but they loved this format, so I continued to use it in other ways. Through the use of games, I was able to go from a boring map-coloring assignment to a full-blown classroom world war. The students could not get enough.

Creating a healthy competition was also a method I used to build student motivation in reading. In all schools, literacy is an area of focus for which teachers scramble to identify tricks to help students focus. Like all teachers, I use research-based academic strategies and would always differentiate my instruction based on the needs of my learners. In this case, I needed the students to read a primary-source document on the Cuban missile crisis during the Cold War, but often my students did not get fired up about reading. I told them to be prepared because we were going to do what Mr. A loves the most. Every single student said, "A competition!"

For the warm-up, students read two pages of the textbook and took notes. Nothing was off limits: students could take as many notes as they wished and they could use what they wrote to help them. I've *never* seen students so attuned to their reading. They were deep into the content and fully immersed in the task. It was exactly what every parent, administrator, and teacher hopes for, a classroom filled with students truly engaged in their learning.

Can we do that again?

When the warm-up was over, I put the students into groups and first told them to quietly but quickly discuss the reading and take any additional notes they thought they would need to remember. Now students were collaborating and discussing the importance of the document, which is key for content retention. After an allotted time working together, I told them we were going to play a game called info hunt. I scrolled down my list of questions, and the student groups had to hunt down the answers in the reading and write them on a whiteboard. The first group to find each answer received two points, and everyone else that got the correct answer within five seconds of the fastest team would get one point. After only three questions, they were going crazy hunting down answers from the primary-source document. They were having fun, totally engaged, and most importantly, learning. The next day, I had multiple students from all my classes ask me, "Can we do that again?" As a teacher, those are the most powerful words a student can say. Playing games does not diminish learning; it enhances engagement and makes learning fun.

Another example of using competition to enhance vocabulary and literacy in the classroom is a game commonly known as headbands. It's a simple game that can ignite a love of learning, is fun, and does not take much effort to set up. Each day I go through new content and I write the new important vocabulary terms on note cards. I hold the note cards above my head, and students have to give me clues as fast as they can. Each time we practice I tell them to give me the clues a bit faster. Once my students get the hang of it, understand the terms, and are quick to give me good definition clues, we set up another competition.

I pit my classes against one another to see which class can go through the vocabulary cards the fastest. We do this every day for a week, and I posted the fastest time in my room on a big scoreboard. Every class runs in and immediately checks who has the fastest time. Sometimes I take it a step further and tell classes that if they work extra hard on the assignment for the day, I will give them extra chances at the end of class to get the best time. You should see the students, on the edge of their seats, fully engaged in a simple vocabulary game. Each class ends with students screaming in enjoyment once I announce their fastest time for the day.

The classroom experience goes to the next level with increased literacy engagement and enhanced content knowledge from the competitive atmosphere. But the most powerful results of academic strategies like a vocabulary competition are the smiling students and, best of all, the question on their lips: "Can we do this again tomorrow?"

Everyday Enthusiasm

Let's be honest, you cannot be exciting every day. In my class I still use worksheets just like every teacher. Sometimes you have to drill the learning objective or help the students learn basic principles. Sometimes an activity using basic note cards is the best teaching tool for your students to retain something. But if you bring enthusiasm to class every day, your students will do worksheets without batting an eye because they love your class. Even when things don't feel fun, they respect the fact that you find new ways to make learning fun. The solution to combating boring lessons is to find a balance. Take every opportunity and look for ways to make activities exciting when you can.

Maybe even more important is taking every opportunity to make competitions into teachable moments, even when students feel like they haven't won. The tears that come from losing can be a powerful motivator for students and can make them work harder to become more successful. Have a real conversation about how in life some people win and some people lose. Emphasize that school gives them an opportunity to win and that you value their hard work.

Whether it's tears or smiles, all feedback is important to a teacher. When I see my students happy and laughing, I know it means they are listening. Students yelling loudly during a race activity means they care. Tears, excitement, laughter, and smiles should all be part of the classroom. If students look like zombies, sitting emotionless, are they really engaged? Are they learning? Are they retaining the information? I would rather have a room filled with emotions because those emotions verify that my students care, and that they are paying attention. In those moments they shared with you, school was fun, it mattered, and it was important.

You Are Not Alone

I'll never forget when someone said to me, "I don't envy you at all. I'm glad I'm not a teacher. I mean, you have to get students to listen to you every single day, and that's exhausting." I love teaching, it is so fulfilling and rewarding. However, I completely agree that it is difficult to capture the hearts and minds of students and to do it every day. Teaching is tough, it's a grind, and it has to happen every single day. Sometimes you just do not know what to do.

It's easy to come up with a perfect Pinterest-ready lesson plan on Monday, maybe even Tuesday. But what about next Tuesday? What about the rest of the school year? It's easy to throw a lesson idea on social media and look like the Teacher of the Year. But sometimes it's difficult to sustain high levels of engagement for long durations because you run out of ideas. Don't worry, this is normal. No matter how great you are with technology or lesson planning, eventually you will need help coming up with engaging and innovative ways to hype your students up.

Collaboration between teachers within a school is underused in education. When I'm struggling, I do not hesitate to talk to my fellow teachers. I will not pretend that I am some sort of wizard of teaching, that I can whip up ideas for lesson plans that are ahead of their time at a moment's notice. I need help just as much as anyone, and when I do, I ask the amazing team of teachers at my school. I work with some of the best teachers in the world, and whether they are in my content area or not, I will ask what kinds of things they do in their class. I can use anything from any subject and find a way to incorporate it into my teaching. I do not stop there; I reach out to other teachers on social media for new ideas that I would never have thought of myself. When it comes to generating a classroom culture that excites students, you don't have to spend hours online searching the depths of Pinterest or spend your entire bank account on teacherspayteachers.com.

This is perhaps one of the most important tips: teachers are a team. We are in this together.

To ensure we are taking every opportunity to reach our students, we must create ways for families to have access to the content we teach and think of innovative approaches to provide those resources. Elementary teacher Andrea Castro began offering math classes for parents with the intention of providing them an opportunity to help their children at home: "I wanted to help create an environment in which they felt secure and comfortable helping their kids at home. They started to see the challenges and victories that their children go through, in addition to better understanding the curriculum. I quickly realized that they were helping me just as much. Their questions and thoughts truly added another layer to my instruction and pushed me to continue reflecting on my teaching. The relationships that were being formed between my families and myself began to change my mindset from 'What can I do?' to 'What can we do?'" Providing opportunities for increased parent involvement not only enhances student growth but also establishes a community feeling of family within the school itself.

Getting to the Next Level

The smallest changes to boring instruction can ignite a fire of engagement in your classroom. Spend ten minutes at the end of class doing something fun—it may not always be academic. I play a game called the tower of terror where I stack four cups on top of each other upside down separated by a simple note card. I compete against the students to see who can get the most cups to fall without the entire tower tipping over. Some teachers might call that a waste of academic time or say that teachers need to focus on standards-based learning every second. I see it as the most powerful ten minutes of the class. In those ten minutes, I gain over an hour of student engagement and focus for the next week.

Look at your instructional strategies, look at what you already use, and try to make it exciting using simple tricks. This is what next-level teaching is all about. Don't re-invent the wheel. The wheel is already there. Just stick it in the car and drive! Don't think you have to spend hours planning the most revolutionary activities each night; most of us don't have time for that. We need simple solutions that yield great returns, and the best way to do this is to look at what we already do and think, "How can I make this better?"

We can all give a damn.

One idea is to use the game Bingo as a fun review activity. In traditional Bingo, you use a Bingo card and place game pieces on the card if a number on your board matches the number the game host calls out, with the goal of completing a line of numbers and yelling, "Bingo." To bring Bingo into my teaching, one day I simply lined my classroom floor with tape and told the students there were no worksheets; the floor was now a Bingo card, and they were the human game pieces.

I divided my students into two teams. I provided all the answers to my clues on pieces of paper, and the students would place those answers on the floor in any box they wished. Students would stand off to the side, and when I gave a clue, they had ten seconds to find the answer on their Bingo card, and someone from the team would stand on that space. As the activity went on, students were collaborating, and engagement was through the roof. My students were smiling, engaged in discussing the content, and moving around the room. Active learning ignites the brain, so get students moving. All I did was tweak an everyday review activity to get students excited and loving school. Think of the instructional strategies you use and how you could change them to create a contagious classroom environment. This is exactly what I did with human Bingo. It didn't take me hours to plan, and it was simple, effective, and highly engaging. That is what next-level teaching is all about.

By creating an environment of fun through competitions, games, races, or even "wasted time," you can establish a learning atmosphere full of enthusiasm. Next-level teaching can just mean adding a little something more to an activity you already use to make it exciting. Take an inside-the-box idea and use an outside-the-box approach, like headbands for vocabulary review or map wars. Use your own flair to create something different, something special. The students will feed off the energy you bring to the class, so make sure to bring energy every day and let the students see it in your instruction, even in small ways. The best part about increasing student engagement is that it is simple and easy tricks can ignite your students' passion for learning.

I don't think anyone can say it better than my favorite teacher, so I'll let him have the last word:

> What do we want to see in our schools? Don't we want to see students eager to learn, excited about what the day holds? Every day is surely not going to be all games and laughter. But neither should it be dull. The truest educator certainly needs a personality that can relate to young people, and they had better have a tireless drive to motivate their kids to use their own talents to tackle some hard, and yes, even boring things, and to stretch themselves to the limit in becoming all they can be.
>
> As a former teacher who taught for over thirty years, I cannot more strongly stress the need to get out of one's comfort zone. Think outside of the box for what you want the students to push themselves to do and be. I could go on and on about strategies or particular lessons or moments. Not all seem like they are a part of your basic curriculum. But can't we take five or ten minutes, or

maybe more, to grab the interest of some young person and sell them on the content? Can't we gain their trust and show that we indeed care about them?

Looking back, I had some wild moments myself. Usually twice during the year, I would have root beer floats to start class. Did that cost me money? Of course it did. Did it teach about World War I and trench warfare? No way! I do not believe the French were making root beer floats in their trenches. But it hooked the students' attention onto what we were going to learn that day. We showed kids that we cared and that our class was a bit different. We had some fun playing music to begin and end a day, with some real dancing going on in the hall. This was to create a fun learning environment where students began to look at school in a more positive light.

I created a village drawn on a twenty-foot piece of paper as seen from a bird's eye view with homes for kids to move into on streets named Adele Alley or Big Bang Avenue. It was nothing big, but we incorporated village life into class, giving out community awards and parking tickets for fun. It gave students an outside-the-box incentive to get them to be a little more motivated that day, to work harder, and to complete more homework. Did it take time to create this? Of course, but it was worth it. Students worked harder so they could move into a bigger house and get a better job. It's similar to what life is truly like, and this also allowed me to have conversations about what life can bring you if you work for it.

Think what can you do to make school a place where a kid can actually make great memories and find the motivation to become more successful. Well, we can all give a damn. We can believe in the power of the individual to stretch imaginations. It is time to put up or shut up. It's time to create something different, something special.

John Alsheimer (Retired Teacher)
South Seneca Central School District

Takeaways

- Student engagement is one of the most powerful forces in a school.
- Students' emotions—their excitement and joy—are the result of the learning environment you create.
- Teachers who want to sustain a high level of engagement in their classrooms should collaborate with fellow teachers and reach out for help.

Next-Level Discussion

How could you enhance your instructional strategies to make them more engaging, and how would those next-level adjustments increase student engagement and improve student learning?

Chapter Five

Storming the Castle: Potential Is Not a Number

A big part of my academic philosophy is built around a quote I have posted on my classroom door for the past few years: "I don't care about grades. I care about effort! If the answer is wrong, don't give up, and don't stop. Make it the best wrong answer I've ever seen."

These are powerful words for students to hear, and they will create a complete shift in the minds of those you teach, especially as they come to realize that they are, perhaps for the first time, meeting a teacher that doesn't care about test grades. My students often say, "Mr. A, please don't be mad at me, but I've never studied for any test in my whole life, but I study for your tests."

If you want your students to be and remain motivated, to work harder for you than they do

for any other teacher, if you want your students to put forth an effort that even they will openly admit they have never made before, then open their eyes to what truly matters to you.

More Than a Test Score

When I first introduce this profound alternative educational philosophy on grades to my students, I don't shy away from its origin, which is my time as a failing student. That's right: the most influential lesson I ever learned about being a successful teacher I learned as a failing student. When I was in school, I was the nice student who would help anyone with anything. I didn't get in trouble. I was kind to everyone, and I worked hard in school. I was never the student who didn't care or fell asleep in the back of class. I was the kind of student that all of us have, who works as hard as they can, who always does their homework, who always completes classroom assignments. I routinely got good grades on homework and always finished projects.

I was that student.

But I struggled to do well on tests. I struggled even though I studied harder than anybody. I took notes, I studied, I thought I had it. But come test day, like clockwork, I would overthink problems or forget simple information that I was able to recite by heart the night before. Once I became aware I wasn't doing well, my nervousness would overtake me even more. I continuously got below-average grades on tests and quizzes. I became frustrated and soon found myself struggling to stay motivated. I remember the year I gave up on school. I stopped caring, hardly did my homework, and didn't pay attention in class. I had become utterly frustrated that no matter how nice I was, how kind and respectful I was, how hard I worked, or how well I did on classwork, it was my test score that the teacher cared about.

When I walked into different classrooms, I began to feel that I was marked as a failure before a new unit even began. My teachers began to see me as a number, as data. I remember teachers hardly working with me because they felt it was more important to work with the students they thought could not only pass but also get high scores. I was viewed as a pass or worse, a fail. I began to believe what I felt my teachers were thinking: that I was a failure and that I didn't matter as much as students who would get As. I remember a teacher telling me I was stupid and another teacher saying I wouldn't amount to much. I can't begin to describe what that did to me. To this day I carry a chip on my shoulder because of this, and I will fight for every student I have because *I was that student!*

Honoring Effort

One of the biggest problems in education is the outdated ideology that test scores are the most important part of education, a notion that has ingrained itself in the minds of educators across the nation. State exams and summative assessments are how we measure student growth, student retention of content knowledge, and a school's academic success. The tests themselves, however, are not the problem. The idea that data and test scores are paramount in education is the problem, and many teachers find themselves forced to continuously fight against this dangerous mind-set.

Teachers have begun to see a shift in schools due to the importance placed on test scores. We see school administrators and teachers focused solely on students passing exams. Because of the pressure put upon teachers, students are, in some cases, seen only as numbers. These numbers are sufficient for the eyes of the state or department of education, which uses them to determine whether our schools are good enough. But these numbers are associated with the worth of a child.

These external pressures may affect the principal. The principal's views may become the views of the staff, and the views of the staff may become the views of the students. I know this firsthand because when I was a student, the way I viewed myself was a direct result of how my teachers and the staff at my school viewed me. Regardless of where these mind-sets begin—principal, parent, community, or teacher—they can influence the success of our students. Teachers' view of students will affect students' motivation, their effort, and perhaps their future. Intentionally or unintentionally, this happens quite often, and it has the potential to create a devastating academic collapse, because once students realize they are just a number, they quit.

It is our job as teachers to eliminate this cycle. Teachers need to help students feel loved, appreciated, and able to build and retain a desire to work hard. I openly defy the norms of education and state quite boldly: I don't care about grades. I care about *effort*.

Help Not Handouts

Another important truth is that grades do matter. They are very important, but tests are not the end result of anything. What the rest of a student's life looks like is the end result. Students won't get and keep jobs because they got an A on an American history test or a math quiz. Students will keep a job because they have been taught to give their job everything they've got, because they learned that putting effort in is the most important thing and that they need to have a never-give-up attitude. That's the mind-set we teachers need to instill in our students. If we foster those beliefs in our students, eventually they will get it, and eventually their test scores will become better. The students will improve. I can attest to this because it's exactly how my story played out.

When I first posted the image of my classroom door with the quote about grades on social media, I received an unbelievable amount of support from teachers all around the world. However, some teachers questioned my teaching philosophy, asking if I just give out trophies. They asked if I go to a doctor who was a D+ student. But they missed the mark. I do not give out trophies, and I'm utterly against handouts. At our school and in my classroom, I tell students that the world is unforgiving and they have to have the heart of a lion, they have to be hungry for success, they have to *earn it!*

Grades are important. I care about grades. All teachers care about grades, but they can have a cost. I don't want students to shut down because they think I don't care about them if they don't get an A. That mind-set is toxic and devastating to a student's future. It's a result of students not receiving sufficient positive reinforcement from the teachers they look up to, and it can lead to students eventually giving up, even if—because of their struggles—they work harder than anyone in their class. That's what happens when students feel like teachers label them as failures or not as important as other students. They internalize thoughts about how they are less worthy, and the urge to quit becomes overwhelming.

Our job as teachers is to do the opposite of this, to build students up. We must make them feel like they matter as long as they give us their best effort. We will not give them a grade that they don't deserve, but no matter their test score, as long as they've done everything to the best of their ability, we will still be proud of them. Our job is to make students believe in themselves and show them that we value what they can do if they try.

Success out of Struggle

Nobody wants to hear about someone who always had it easy with a perfect life. The best success stories involve monumental struggles. The failures are what make the successes worth hearing about. J. K. Rowling's writing was rejected by publishers countless times before she became celebrated for one of the greatest book series in the world, Harry Potter. Walt Disney struggled to get a foothold in the film industry before succeeding. Abraham Lincoln was, by all accounts, a failure at many things early on in his life before he became president of the United States of America.

It's not where you start
that counts;
it's where you finish!

I love sharing the story of Dwayne "The Rock" Johnson, a famous professional wrestler and actor who once epitomized someone who fell to the bottom. As The

Rock puts it, he had dreams of playing professional football, getting rich, and living a dream life. However, he was cut from a Canadian professional football team and had to move back in with his parents. He recalled how when he was cut from the team, he had only seven dollars in his pocket and no idea what to do next. As we now know, he ended up becoming a world-famous wrestler and award-winning actor who owns his own production company.

These stories are fascinating now because we see these names and recognize them for the amazing achievements they've accomplished. But they're important because students need to know the truth of the struggle. That's why I don't shy away from talking about my academic background and struggles when I explain my unusual ideology as it relates to student grades. I was a student who was once called stupid and who teachers thought would become nothing, and I have been a Teacher of the Year; worked with the UFC, celebrities, sports agents, professional athletes, clothing brands, television and movie directors and producers; owned my own business; and authored a book. Do not tell my students they cannot achieve greatness, and do not tell me that a test score identifies the potential of any of my students.

When speaking to my students, I tell them I know that it's easy to get lost in the detrimental mind-set that says they can't make anything happen, but that success in anything is just on the other side of hard work. They have to push negativity out of their minds and get over the natural proclivity to think that they are going to fail. If they are determined to make it happen, anything is possible. There is always more to us than what others see, and there is a strength that gives us the ability to take on any challenge. It is up to us to decide how we want to take on that challenge.

Once I became a teacher, I realized just how important my attitude toward my students was. I realized that everything I did would be internalized by my students: the words I said to them, how I acted toward them, how my thoughts played out. Those same students would either live out the same challenges I'd had to live with, or they would find success. Either way, I decided what my attitude would be as their classroom teacher. I refused to let anybody—teacher, parent, or principal—dictate how I would view my students. My views could become their thoughts, and their thoughts could become their reality. For this reason, I refused to see my students as data.

There is another quote taped on my door which has become the motto for my classroom. The quote came from a mixed martial arts T-shirt, and it is "Kings aren't born in castles." That statement together with my ideology on grades helps my classroom be a place where students work hard. "Kings aren't born in castles" is a statement reflecting that success takes hard work; effort is the determining factor because no one is born being good at anything.

I see teaching as full of opportunities. One opportunity I won't pass up is the chance to show my students that school is not about a test; it is about learning to overcome any obstacle. I tell my students if they want something in life, they have to earn it.

Walk into my classroom tomorrow and ask my students, "What's the number one word in this room?"

All my students will say, "Effort."

Putting Grades in Context

As teachers, we have a responsibility to use our platforms to educate students about life and establishing a work ethic. I openly ask my students, "How are you preparing for the future?" Then I tell them that they're either preparing themselves for something great or preparing for a life they're going to hate. "But make no mistake," I say, "you are preparing for something."

Those conversations are powerful because my students hear my expectations about hard work and effort. The understanding that I want them to meet my expectations is how I get the most effort from them. If we want our students to be successful, we have to create the space for them to be successful. That is why I tell my students that the end result is not the test at the end of the unit. The end result is not the state exam at the end of the school year. The end result is what the rest of their lives are going to look like.

If we let our students shut down because they get poor test scores, we may alter their future. We need them to think that if they want something, they have to give us their best effort and work as hard as humanly possible. They must complete every assignment to the best of their ability. If we see that they are trying, who cares what their test score is? If they did their very best, we should be high-fiving them and praising them—whatever their score. If you praise them for their effort, students will work hard for you. At that moment, you become that teacher that they will always remember. All it takes is one moment to build a positive relationship.

On day one with my students, I make it perfectly clear what my expectations are. These conversations are a must. They drill home that effort and motivation are more important than any grade on a test. From that moment on, students give me everything they have. Classwork, homework, and projects are completed. Students show me they are going above and beyond. When it comes to tests, students are determined to prove to me just how hard they work. To them, the most important thing is to prove to Mr. Alsheimer they are working as hard as they can, and they do. I've had students show me letters from their parents stating that they were studying at home and quizzing themselves. I've had students show me screenshots on their phones from group texts about questions from their stacks of flash cards. The motivation they had, to prove to me they were working hard, was exponentially greater than if I had just been pushing students to get an A on the test.

Results that Matter

The end result isn't the test . . . what's the *rest of their life* gonna look like? That's the end result.

When you start praising students' efforts, you will see the greatest amount of change in their work. You will see higher results on your unit exams because of the increase in completed work.

I know this because when I first employed this effort-first attitude, I soon found myself in the midst of the highest test results I had ever seen. Across all my classes the scores were incredible. Students told me time and time again how they had never studied for anything until they came to my class. I had students openly and proudly stating that they did not do homework or study for any other teacher but me.

One student who had failed everything in the first two months of school, as well as many of his state exams in years past, finally turned the corner. He started bringing a notebook to class each day and started doing his homework and classwork. He was determined to prove to me that he was studying, but even so, I could tell he still thought he would fail our unit test on immigration. The day of the test, I pulled him aside and told him that I had noticed every bit of effort he had put in and that after the test was over I would still be proud of him, no matter what grade he got.

He finished the test, and I was nervous for him. I kept thinking, "Please be anything but a low grade." He deserved so much more than a below-average score for the time he put in. He looked worried as we went over the answers to the test. As we discussed each question, the fear that he was going to hear bad news yet again was all over his face.

But he didn't. He earned a 100 percent on a unit test for the first time in his life. He was floored; he could not believe he had finally done it. I cheered for him in front of the entire class and told him how proud I was that he had given me everything he could. Since that day, he has never looked back and has given me his very best all the time. He studies his heart out for every test and still gets amazing scores on exams.

By praising effort, you give students so much support, which leads to stronger relationships. Just like when I was a student, it will eventually click. I went from being a below-average student to a 4.0 student in graduate school.

Getting to the Next Level

Education isn't about a score on some history test. Superintendent Steve Zielinski offers this advice: "The key is to value your students; hold them to high standards without making them feel like you don't approve of who they are."

58

NEXT-LEVEL TEACHING

My students are not defined by a letter or a number on a page, just as I was not defined by my grades. Yes, tests are important, and we all want our students to get great grades. But what's more important is building relationships, helping our students to learn to work as hard as they can, and understanding that success must be earned. Kings aren't born in castles.

If they do all of those things and still get a D+, praise them for everything they did leading up to that moment. Wipe away the tears of frustration from their eyes and tell them that they demonstrated something far greater than the grade they got. They showed heart, determination, and a never-surrender attitude. They are something far greater to you than a pass rate.

As the classroom teacher, you can change the minds of the students. Perhaps for the first time in their lives, your students will put forward their best efforts—because that was what you told them was most important. And when the dust settles, whether they get As on their tests or not, you'll tell them that they matter. You might change their future because you were the first person in their life to look at them differently. You might be the only person that told them you were proud of them.

You just might end up being *that teacher—the one they always remember, because you told them it's not where you start that counts, it's where you finish.*

Takeaways

- A class built around effort, not test scores, will actually result in increased test scores.
- Tell your stories of failure to connect with your students. Your success story is only worth hearing because of your struggle, and students will identify with that struggle.
- Share stories of celebrities who were at one point considered failures. This opens the eyes of students going through similar problems, both academic and personal.

Next-Level Discussion

Think of a few ways you could go to the next level to make your students feel like they are more than a test score.

Part Two

Teacher Outlook

Chapter Six

Thinking Outside the School Box

As professional educators, we take risks every day. We work in situations that aren't always optimal. Our students deserve the very best schools we can give them, and to truly make our schools amazing, we need to think outside the box and find unconventional methods to enhance the experiences we give them. After all, if we're going to take risks, why not take a risk on making our schools better for the students that need them? So, nothing should be off the table. Use any and all options.

Too often we think we can only do something one way just because that is how it's always been done. But if your idea is good for students, if it's better for your school, then go and do it.

Enter the Dragon

In my love of mixed martial arts, I became a big fan of UFC lightweight contender Paul "The Irish Dragon" Felder. I would say he is my favorite UFC/MMA fighter. I had a family connection through my uncle, so I decided to reach out to him. I had my students make a sign for one of his fights, and we took a picture and tweeted it out, asking him to come to our school. To our surprise, he responded and said, "Tell me when." How cool is that? A celebrity and professional fighter willing to give some students the time of day.

We need to find ways to meet and connect with *all our students.*

This is where my *why-not* approach to life comes in, and where my views on education are very much outside the box. I am always looking for unconventional ways to connect with students. Schools aren't full of the same typical student created on an assembly line with the exact same interests and problems. Each student is different. We need to find unique ways to meet and connect with all our students that will reach them individually and inspire and motivate them to accomplish their goals and chase their dreams.

When Paul Felder came in, he and his manager, Brian Butler, admitted that what they saw was totally different than their wildest expectations of a school. We hadn't set up a traditional presentation. We blew the roof off with a setting that mirrored a UFC event. We didn't have him stand in front of a class or in the cafeteria and talk for five minutes. We created an experience that would hype up the crowd, hype up our presenter, and hype up the staff. We blacked out the gymnasium, had flashing lights, blasted loud music, and pumped in fog. I created a one-minute video similar to a sports promo with highlights from Paul Felder's career, and we showed it on a big screen while blasting epic theme music. We set up wrestling mats in the middle of the gym, and packed it full of students. We simulated a UFC introduction with an announcer, a teacher—Matthew Schaffer—whose style was similar to Bruce Buffer, a legendary announcer for the UFC. Paul put on a martial arts display, kicking and punching pads, doing martial arts combinations, and calling faculty and students to join in. It was incredible.

Once we had the students hooked, I took the mic and interviewed Paul. Our presentation wasn't about fighting; it was about accomplishing goals. It was about grit, determination, goal setting, and fighting for your dreams. We talked about how he set everything aside and focused solely on capturing his desired outcome when training for a big fight, much like students need to do before a big test. We talked about how he loved drama and theater and had even studied those subjects in college. He showed the students that even tough guys can have a love of learning. Most of all, we discussed hard work, effort, and his profound antibullying message.

Many of our male students who had a history of disciplinary issues, along with many other students who were fascinated with Paul's story, wanted to take pictures with him. They thought it was so cool that someone who fights in front of millions of people on television would fly hundreds of miles to come speak to them in a small middle school. Our why-not mentality had turned a seemingly impossible task of connecting with someone only seen on television into a reality.

I know many would have said, "Why even try? He won't come."

But he did. And together we created one of the coolest days in our school's history.

Too Cool for Bullying

We didn't stop there. In my brief but exciting MMA fighting career, I made connections with a clothing brand called Fear the Fighter. I got in touch with them to create an antibullying campaign and T-shirt for our school. The idea behind the project was to find an alternative, extreme, and cool way to bring students' attention to a disturbing epidemic sweeping the nation. Many people viewed my idea as controversial at first, like they had when I'd asked a UFC fighter to come speak at our school. To some, calling upon a fight-oriented clothing brand that sponsors professional fighters and former UFC champions to campaign against bullying seemed contradictory and negative. But I knew that trying something new and fresh could yield powerful results.

We created an in-your-face message with an inside-the-box idea using an outside-the-box approach, and we had students asking daily how they could get one of those cool T-shirts. And the message came through. We saw students standing up for other students in classes and in the halls. There was a school-wide increase in random acts of kindness. The simple idea of kindness became cool. A T-shirt doesn't change a bully, but it can bring attention to a powerful idea. Change what's cool, and you change the bully. Sending a message of kindness and hope in a unique way can affect a student who might otherwise never have been reached.

Our small, unorthodox project quickly turned global. Schools all around the world were buying the T-shirt and buying into the message that started with Hamish Brewer, Chad Elliot, and myself. An idea that many would have rejected became a trendy new movement in the world of education.

Transformative Threads

The school that I work in has an extremely high poverty rate with many at-risk students and students in need. I had noticed that many of our students wore the same clothing all year long. I knew, too, that some of the students struggled with depression and thoughts of suicide. I wanted to create something that would help students in need and help any student who wanted to become a leader or wanted to work hard, not only at schoolwork but also in building character.

I knew the time to change the future was right now, so I started to think of ways to attack this problem beyond the call of the ordinary classroom teacher. In every struggle throughout my career, I have looked for ways to adapt and to bring change. I look for ways to better my school and continue to build a positive school environment for every student who walks through our doors. In this case, I decided to go after something big, something that, to my knowledge, no school had ever done: partner with a clothing brand so big they can be found at any mall in America.

I wanted to find a company that would provide us with clothes that would help our students in need and also look cool enough that every student would want to work hard to earn them. I knew it would have to be a clothing brand that students would like. The problem was connecting a teacher from a small middle school in northern Virginia with a big-time clothing line. That was a task that would seem insurmountable to many. Most educators wouldn't even dare to try. But that's not my mind-set. I know that you must believe that no challenge is too big to try and no obstacle will make you give up. Because, quite simply, giving up is quitting on your students.

I used every social media outlet I could: Twitter, Instagram, Facebook. I sent emails and made phone calls. All summer long I was sent and resent messages. No matter how many times I heard the word no, I was determined to make something special happen. Finally, a company based in Los Angeles answered the call. Chris "Drama" Pfaff, a reality television star who created the clothing brand Young and Reckless, gave us more than we could have asked for. I sent out a mass email to the school staff asking for students who were leaders in the classroom or who were good decision makers to come to my classroom for a Young and Reckless shirt. Before I knew it, there were students all over the school rocking the gear, and I had lines of students outside my door asking, "How do I get a shirt?"

Suddenly, more students were seeking out ways to go the extra mile in class, to stand out, and to be leaders. We had students studying who said they normally didn't study. They all wanted to be a part of something bigger, to be a part of a movement that began with a teacher saying, "Why not?"

To be honest, I must have heard the word no from over twenty brands before Young and Reckless responded with a yes. *Ninety-nine nos and one yes is still a YES! Why not go for broke? Why not go after every opportunity for your students? In this case it created success far beyond what I originally imagined.*

Complacency Kills

Teachers must be willing to use every possible network to connect with people. Social media is a great way to connect with stakeholders that might have seemed out of your reach. Use it to establish a connection with people and companies, from your local community to celebrities you see on television. From there, tell your school's story and do not give up.

Social media can negatively affect people, but it can also be an untapped resource for something good. Through social media, our school was able to connect with a local business that specialized in fitness. From there, we utilized TeacherFit, a website and app that gives teachers access to a health and wellness program. I used the program as an incentive for my mentoring group to work out after school. Empowering students through physical fitness and nutritional awareness, building relationships, and shaping student character all started through social media and through direct contact with local business owners.

So send emails and direct messages and continue to make connections with the local community and with other schools and teachers. When reaching out to new resources, if you do not hear back immediately, continue working. You did not give up learning to read after you had difficulty sounding out the first word, and this is no different. If your school needs more technology, flexible seating, resources, or athletic equipment, reach out and get it. Nobody will give you anything if you don't ask, so go ask.

I received the best advice from Chris "Drama" Pfaff. During a Skype conversation between Hamish Brewer, Drama, and myself, I asked Drama for any advice he could give to other teachers and educators looking to connect with big brands. He said, "Using all social media outlets and creativity are key." So do things like producing your own creative videos to capture the attention of the audience you wish to connect with. That might mean becoming proficient at using iMovie and becoming a scriptwriter, producer, and director in your free time. When it comes to making your school environment and culture amazing, nothing should be off the table.

The most important thing for teachers to realize is that the environment of a school is created with the work they are willing to put in. From getting a UFC fighter to speak to our students to working with an MMA clothing company to establish an antibullying campaign to partnering with a multimillion-dollar clothing line created by a reality television star, began with my why-not mentality. I was driven to accept challenges and to believe that there was nothing our school couldn't have.

One of the worst things that can happen in your educational journey is for you to become complacent.

Getting to the Next Level

Remember why you signed up to be a teacher. Remember that you got involved in education because you wanted to change the world. You wanted to change lives. You wanted to be the difference. You began this amazing but difficult journey because you wanted to be that one teacher that your students will remember years later. In order to be that, you must be willing to go beyond the call. Begin to look for the problems and go find answers. Use the local community and social media to find solutions. Create partnerships or start programs within your school that have a lasting impact.

Going beyond the call means you are willing to dig deep and create opportunities for your school in ways that others won't see. The best of us will rise to the occasion and continue to look for something new that will create an incredibly positive school environment. If it's good for students, then it's good for education. Nothing and no one is off the table. Whether it's bringing in a UFC fighter or reaching out to a business in your community to donate school supplies for your students, if they can help you or your school, then go for it.

Takeaways

- Provide students with opportunities and experiences that are unconventional for a normal school and cool in the eyes of students.
- Create interest by telling your school's story so that others will rise to the occasion and join your effort.
- Dig deep and create opportunities for your school in new and unique ways including using social media to make connections and gain new resources.

Next-Level Discussion

Think of a problem specific to your classroom or school. How could you go to the next level to create a solution and provide something positive for your students?

Chapter Seven

Building Bridges

The laundry list of obligations that educators face can be daunting. However, one item must stay atop the list of demands no matter how tired we are or how bad our day has been. This item holds the key to developing the most dynamic school atmosphere: it's building sincere and genuine relationships with students.

But too often, this one task gets lost.

Our job goes beyond academics. Relationships are built on a mutual respect and love for one another. We need to give our students a place without judgment, where they feel comfortable and safe. Powerful and meaningful relationships drive students' positive behavior and influence their academic achievement.

When you build positive relationships, you will see a decrease in classroom disruptions and see a dramatic increase in academic achievement. It's so simple, yet so powerful: educators must show students that they truly care about them. It is the key to unlocking the potential of your classroom. It is also key in taking your school and your teaching to the next level.

There are no
shadows
in education.

Often our students come from amazing families filled with love and support, families who go the extra mile to help and provide for their children. Parents might work multiple jobs and do whatever it takes to make sure their children do not go without. But that is not true in every case. Our students come from a multitude of backgrounds; some are fortunate while some are less fortunate. Some students' experiences would shock and sadden even the toughest of hearts. They come from places where they have no one, where they are alone, where there is no support, and they see and go through things that no child or teenager should have to experience.

The only schools I have worked at in my educational career are at-risk schools with students from a variety of backgrounds. Many have troubling pasts, economic problems, abusive homes, and many are in need of some form of help.

When I first began teaching, I moved from the East Coast to Kansas City, Missouri, and my wife and I took jobs at the same school in the inner city. My wife taught middle school math and science while I taught geography and psychology in the high school. This was at one of the toughest schools in a city with a high gang-affiliation rate, high poverty rate, and a crime rate that was over three times the national average. Students in both middle school and high school had to submit to metal detectors and searches by security guards every morning to ensure everyone's safety. I remember being told that I was the sixth teacher that year to use my classroom. One teacher had quit after one day, another after a week. Here I was, taking over a class midway through the year, walking into a hostile situation with students who had not had a stable teacher all year. I was just trying to survive in the world of teaching, all while working in one of the toughest schools in Kansas City.

I remember talking with my students about their lives and getting to know them. One particular student made me rethink some of my philosophies of education. That student's name was Marvin Clark II.

He was a quiet student who had a calm demeanor and was never disrespect-ful. I remember him as a student who loved basketball. I still recall when we played a staff-versus-student game and how difficult it was to guard him—even when he was only in tenth grade.

What I didn't know at the time were the struggles he had in his life, struggles that made so many other students quit and fall into a life of gangs, drugs, and violence. I later learned that Marvin moved around a lot. Sometimes his fam-ily struggled to find a place to stay; sometimes he lived in shelters. He grew up seeing a lot of violence at a young age and experiencing situations and problems that no kid should. With all this struggle in his life, he still came to school, and we still had positive interactions.

Most people—students especially—find ways to hide their pain. We often don't want people to know when we are going through difficult times. I came to work and struggled to focus; my mom was battling cancer and just trying to survive. I didn't share that story very often, and in fact, most people had no idea what my family was going through. Many of our students face similar situations or worse daily.

Looking back, what I struggle with the most is what I might have missed. How could I have not seen the pain Marvin was dealing with? How did I miss his struggle? Now more than ever, I see the value in how teachers interact with students. Early in my career, I thought teaching was about content. Marvin's story and so many others have taught me that while instruction and content are important, our students' lives and the relationships we build with them are more important. So often a student is carrying the weight of the world on their shoulders. What are we doing to lift them up, to ease the weight? What are we doing to help them?

Marvin went on to play division I basketball. He graduated from college and now plays professional basketball. I was lucky enough to see him play in front of thousands of fans. I screamed at the top of my lungs in excitement when he hit a big three-pointer near the end of the game. Marvin rose to accomplish his dreams through hard work and a desire to succeed in life. His story is powerful, and it's a reminder that the baggage students bring to school is not their fault and that we as educators can sometimes be light and energy in a day that might be filled with despair and frustration. In that small window we have with a student, can we give them the love we would want our own child to be given?

Affirmation Is the Key

An amazing school culture starts with the leaders of the school, but it is built inside the classroom. Kings aren't born in castles, and schools are not simply successful on their own; we have to make them that way. The best opportunity we have for success in our schools is to get involved with students.

I have often talked with students and asked what they think the biggest problems in school are. Almost every time they give the same answer: the biggest problems are the teachers who act like they are only there for a paycheck, which is as funny as it sounds, because anyone involved in education knows that educators make very little money.

What students are describing is the kind of teacher who shows up, gives them a worksheet to shut them up, barks orders, treats the class punitively, and makes no attempt at creating a connection with students in the classroom. We have all seen this kind of teacher. They hesitate to change their teaching style, they're often cynical, and they roll through the halls rarely conversing with anyone. Rather than interacting with students, these teachers practically brush right past them. This is the type of teacher who refuses to go out of their way for the betterment of the school and only bothers to connect with students with high grades. They do not see opportunity but obligation. Think of a child sitting in a home with parents who are screaming or throwing things. Think of a child experiencing abuse. What is the first thing you would do if that child walked into your classroom right now? They might. Doesn't that speak to how much power we hold? Remember, you're not just an educator. When students see we care about the details of their lives, they will allow us to have a much larger impact on their future. Relationships are the difference. That is the key to unlocking unlimited potential in our students. Just think how schools would be different if all teachers and educators thought like that.

One year our school did an experiment with rice. We took two identical jars of rice and we put one jar in a room on one side of the school and the other jar on the other side of the school. Every day for a month, we spoke nicely to one jar of rice and we spoke negatively to the other. We would say things like, "Rice, you're so smart and beautiful. I bet you taste so good." While the other rice would hear, "You're so stupid, rice. I hate you!" Over time, we saw a difference in the appearance of the rice. The rice we spoke positively to looked much better than the rice we spoke negatively to.

Whether or not rice truly reacts to how we speak, think of how students are affected. If we want to build positive relationships with our students, it begins with each interaction. Our attitude and mind-set can play a major role in our ability to build meaningful relationships. Our attitude can help an unsuccessful student bridge the gap to become a successful student. A student will try just a little bit harder for *that teacher* who forged a bond with them, no matter the outcome. It is no secret that some students will shut down immediately for some teachers, while the same students will run through a brick wall for another. It all comes down to the relationship and environment we create.

Although simple in concept, relationship building is difficult to execute with precision and consistency. In my journey in education I have seen many teachers obtain relationships with certain kinds of students or a given group or grade level but not others. How do we make an impact across grade levels and across the school? How do we make it so every student knows our name and will follow us not because they sit in our class, but because we have established something more powerful, a lasting impression?

You're Not Their Friend

I have heard teachers new to the field explain how much they love teaching, how easy their classes are, and how much fun school is in October. When you see this teacher in the halls, they are over-the-top, acting as a friend to their students rather than as a mentor and an educational professional. This is not a positive relationship with students. It's the result of the flawed thinking of an inexperienced teacher. Students do not need you to be their friend. This approach does not create lasting bonds or relationships built on respect. More importantly, it's not effective for education. These teachers are overwhelmed by December. Their students will not seek guidance or mentorship from them. When students do not have respect for you, they will not learn from you.

The best way to establish relationships with students is to first take on a supportive role. Students need boundaries and structure, so provide that for them. Do not make the mistake of jumping too high too fast. The process will take time. Do not push or rush it, for respect must be established first. Still, even though you may be stern on day one, look for every opportunity to make one-on-one connections with your students. Relationships and next-level teaching take time, but they give you an ability to wield a powerful influence later.

When you take on a supportive role, you provide structure in students' chaotic world and you offer your students something they are yearning for. Students need people to look up to. Many come from broken homes, and they are looking specifically for parental figures. By establishing a classroom built around this model, you offer your students a safe zone that they may not have at home, a sanctuary of consistency. You also wield something else. For the students who do not come from great families, you have taken the opportunity to be the missing link in their life. You may be the only person in their life who cares about how they are doing and worries about their well-being. Don't ever underestimate the power of being there. You may just be the most important face in the crowd.

Your students know—no matter what took place yesterday, no matter how loud their parents screamed at each other last night, no matter which person in their life let them down once again—once they cross the doorstep of your classroom you will be there, smiling and genuinely happy to see them. They know when they share a story, you are actually listening because you care and you are truly proud of them. You'll become *that teacher*, the one they cannot wait to see because they know you cannot wait to see them.

Ensuring Engagement

The next step to building powerful long-lasting relationships with students is engagement. You cannot be the kind of teacher who loves students and takes every opportunity to connect without showing it in your planning and preparation for your classroom. Student engagement allows you to make connections faster and easier, and students will actually begin to engage with you because your class is their favorite. If students enjoy talking with you in the halls but hate walking into your classroom because you are boring, you've limited your ability to influence both that student and your school.

Your goal each and every day should be to create a classroom so welcoming, an atmosphere so exciting, and lessons so engaging that your principal cannot help but smile at all the happy faces they see as they walk past your classroom. Get the students up, moving around, laughing, and so entrenched in content that once the bell rings they say, "Oh man, already?" Positive relationships plus student engagement equal academic success. Make it fun, make it engaging, and make your classroom a place of structure where all students can learn. You now have the formula for student-teacher relationships that other teachers will want to emulate.

Once you have a foundation and have created a classroom culture built on respect and fun, you can extend your influence around the school. With the ability to reach all students, your influence should be felt across classes so every student knows and respects your name. When students in other grade levels see you in the hall, they'll change their behavior because they know you and, perhaps, have begun to build a positive relationship with you as well. They say hello because you are known around the school and not just in your hallway: your influence is felt in all corners of the school building.

Getting on Their Level

One way to make a tremendous impact on students is getting involved in their lives. Once respect has been established, the student knows the boundaries of the relationship. When students respect you and care about you, you can step outside of your comfort zone and they will still understand the boundaries of your relationship.

When a strong student-teacher relationship is being developed, you can use after-school programs, like tutoring, coaching, or clubs, which allows you to get to know students in a different way. You are stepping out of the teacher in the classroom role and you are working with students in a different setting. After-school events are like winning a lottery, and most teachers do not play, so capitalize on it.

In the past I helped run a soccer program with my good friend Matthew Schaffer. For many students from other countries, soccer is much more than a game; it is life. We had some amazing competitions, and a few other teachers and I played with and against the students. We got to compete and also to laugh and have fun with them. It's important that they see adults taking the time to get on their level, being a part of something they enjoy.

Talking with students outside of the realm of academics opens doors to positive relationships. You can become the most important person in the entire school building to a student without even teaching them in a class because, unlike so many others, you are spending time with them. You are there for them with a smile on your face when they know you could be home or doing anything else.

Getting involved outside of the classroom is much more than participating in after-school events. One year during one of our school's spirit weeks, I saw a group of students who weren't participating because they clearly thought it wasn't "cool." I knew it was time to make school more exciting. When Ben Plummer, another teacher, came to me actively wanting to get involved in spirit week and asked if I wanted to join in, I said absolutely. The following day the spirit week theme was to dress up like characters, so we chose characters from the video game Fortnite, which all our students were obsessed with. We went all-out: we dressed up, we took pictures before school, and we posted them around the halls. We wore the costumes all day long as we taught class and walked through

the hallways. We asked students in the halls to vote for us at lunch for coolest outfit and to dress up tomorrow themselves. It did not take long before more and more students got involved and started talking about what they were going to wear the next day—and they actually did get dressed up.

But the impact of that act lasted for weeks later. Both Ben and I had students continue to bring up the fact that we had dressed up and went all-out. One student made a cutout of Ben in his costume and put it in his classroom.

Dressing up gave us common ground to relate to our students. Choosing characters who were not easy to re-create from a video game that all our students played and loved opened opportunities for students to joke around with us, to ask if we play Fortnite, and to bridge the gap between student and teacher. We got students to open up, get more involved, and join the fun.

Getting to the Next Level

Teachers cannot stand off to the side and expect great change to happen. We need to take every opportunity to take our classroom and school to the next level. You, as the classroom teacher, can create a passion and love of learning, motivating your students in a way that only comes from moments of laughter, excitement, and happiness. Your relationships with your students will be so sound that when you have an off day, when you have been up all night with your sick children, or when you feel like you are burned out, your students will come to build you up. They'll ask how you are doing, and a small smile even on a bad day can brighten even the darkest moments.

Move from being just their teacher to being *that* teacher, the one they will go to any lengths to help because you are always there for them. Be there cheering when they succeed, be there listening to their struggles, and be there holding them up when their world is crashing down. These are the moments when you can impact their future and have conversations to make them better people. You can build their love of learning through their respect of you. You can shape their future by disrupting their present and allowing them the chance to take their academic life to the next level.

Takeaways

- Building relationships is not acting like a friend but establishing boundaries and working to make connections.
- Get involved in after-school programs even if that is just going to a sporting event or concert.
- Once a relationship based on respect has been established, find ways to have fun and get on your students' level. Having fun with students allows them to see you as more than just their classroom teacher.

Next-Level Discussion

Consider your daily interactions with your students. How can you go to the next level to get involved in their lives?

Chapter Eight

Heart to Heart

As a young boy I always dreamed of being a star athlete. From the time I was in diapers, my father had me swinging a bat and shooting a basketball. When I was young, I traveled all over, I played in big tournaments, and I always measured myself against the best player on the field. My father always said if I wanted to be good at something, I should play as much as I could and practice how I played. If I had to dive to catch a line drive in a game, I had better dive in practice. Those words from my father altered my future. "Nobody should outwork you" became my motto early on and it has been forged into my work ethic today. I vowed to always be the hardest worker in the room, no matter if I succeed or fail. The one thing I can control is that nobody outworks me.

I found myself traveling to baseball camps at different colleges, and then later playing baseball in college. Eventually I got several opportunities to try out for professional baseball teams. The day before the draft after my senior season, I was invited to an invitation-only last-chance tryout at the stadium of the Rochester Redwings, the Minnesota Twins triple-A affiliate, which is one step below the big leagues. I was standing next to players from some of the biggest colleges in the nation. I can honestly say I felt a little out of my league next to one of the starting players for the University of Florida's baseball team. Regardless, I was sure of one thing: I would make my presence known as the one player the team had to see because I would outwork everyone there. It was one of my best tryouts, and afterward one of the scouts for the Minnesota Twins organization and I had a long conversation about the possibility of me playing for the Twins.

Then draft day came, and I was not picked up by a major league organization. I was crushed.

I was eventually invited to try out for another professional organization. This time, the airline lost my luggage, which had all of my baseball gear. That night I made a name for myself in front of all the scouts and coaches. The only equipment I had for the first practice was a T-shirt, a pair of shorts, sneakers, and my glove, which I had carried on the plane. I had to borrow a bat from another player. One of the scouts came over and asked me if I wanted to sit out until all my gear came the next day. I told him I had not flown all the way there to sit on the sidelines; I was there to get signed to play professional baseball—or go down swinging. Every single scout and coach there told me in a private meeting at the end of the week that I had more heart than any player they had seen in a long time. They said I was one of the final names discussed to get a contract, but they did not offer me one. They wished me luck. I smiled. I felt encouraged that I once again was almost the name picked and every coach saw me as the hardest worker on the field.

But I also felt like I failed. Those ideas I had long ago of being someone important or something grand were beginning to fade. My father's words, however, still rang in my ears. Even if the dream of playing professional baseball would never transpire, I could prove that I would never quit. "Nobody out-works you" is the same mentality that drives me even now, and it will continue to push me throughout my life. So often we hear stories of those with great talent and great potential, but once hardship hits, what do they do then? In my own life story, I refused to be a character who quit or gave anything other than my best.

Life Lessons

I've found that students need to hear about more than just academics from their teachers, and stories provide the teacher with the ability to teach outside the realm of a textbook. You can teach about life. Some students quite simply need to hear these things from someone other than their parents, someone like a teacher whom they respect. Conversations can have a lasting impact on students' lives and ultimately have a profound effect on your school. Students will begin to think differently, act differently, and take education more seriously.

Find the right moment
to give them
hope.

Soon students will come to you for advice, to share a funny story, or to share a moment of success in their lives. Take this time to have deep, meaningful conversations. Teach them about more than just content, teach them about how to be strong men and women.

Stories about our lives are some of the most important opportunities we as teachers can take hold of. Sometimes, long after the school year has begun and I have a firm hold of my students' respect and appreciation, I've spoken openly about my family, about my daughters, my wife, and about my life's successes and struggles. I've spoken about a time in my life when my mother was diagnosed with breast cancer. I've discussed the hardships that came from that and how she has continued to battle multiple occurrences of the disease. Time after time, the cancer has come and gone. I've described seeing my mother's body begin to fade, but her spirit refusing to give up has forged an even deeper work ethic in my soul. Several students who have heard that story through the years have also shared that someone in their life had cancer. On multiple occasions I have shared tears with students about our fears and our hopes.

At other times I have shared stories about my daughter's journey with learning to read. At first, she wanted to quit because it was hard. My wife would work with her on words, and over time she began to get it. She started to improve, and one day her mother and I found her in a corner of the house quietly reading her books to herself. She overcame her struggle through hard work. Students love to hear that teachers are human and that we have much more to talk about than schoolwork. They can be encouraged that our life stories have similarities to theirs, that no one is without struggle, and that we all have the strength to face adversity.

Meaningful Lessons

One day in my classroom I felt the need to start a conversation about life, and I used a few minutes at the end of my class to teach my students a strong and meaningful lesson that they needed to hear. I talked about my life, baseball, and teaching. I said that struggles are faced by everyone, but people are defined by how they handle those struggles. I had the feeling that one of the students that day was a child with the same feelings I once had: someone who worked and worked but for whatever the reason always fell short, which resulted in negative feelings consuming them. I continued to explain that failure is part of life, and struggles are part of success.

Everyone in the room was moved by this lesson. I could see and feel that the students were soaking up every word. Somewhere in their life there were moments of failure or family struggle, and these words were just what they needed. I hoped that they would have an answer the next time they wanted to say, "Why try? I always fail." I aimed to give them the motivation I once needed. I wanted to get them to keep pushing because I knew on the other side of their impossible struggle will be their biggest success.

What I've gained from my own struggles is the ability to connect with so many different kinds of students. I speak about positive relationships and goal setting and how those things can impact their future. I have discussed with the young women how I would want my two daughters to be treated with respect and dignity by any young man; I talk to the young men about how to respect women, how to treat adults, and the importance of conflict resolution. I do all these things in small doses throughout the school year in moments that seem appropriate.

Many times, those moments are at the start of class. At other times, they're at the end of class as my final thought for the day or as something for them to think about over the weekend. Those powerful moments might push a student to work a little harder and graduate, to go on to college, or to overcome a personal or family struggle. Students take inspiration from you, and your stories and life lessons can guide them in times where they feel lost. Your words can live on because they touched just one student's heart.

Reach Beyond the Classroom

As educators our jobs exceed far beyond what is printed on our job descriptions. We have a unique opportunity to change the trajectory of the lives of the students we teach. Many times, simple conversations about life can have a profound impact on a student's future. Find the right moment and move outside the realm of the textbook to discuss something far more powerful than numbers or vocabulary. Talk about life to your students—you may be the only person to do so.

Imagine if teachers in all grade levels began to add a few minutes every now and again to talk about life. How much could that alter the trajectory of a student's story? How could those conversations impact school culture if they led students to think differently? Adrienne Wiggins and Lindsey Le, both elementary teachers, implemented boys and girls mentoring groups, where the focus for each group was to build relationships in a way that was based on the unique needs of the students. The purpose for Girls with Pearls was to give the girls a safe place to interact, be creative, and respond to stories written to celebrate and empower them. Guys with Ties had a male mentor who focused on teaching young men how to make good decisions in everyday situations, like when you lose on the basketball court, how to look someone in the eye, and how to shake their hand properly. Moments like these create powerful waves of influence on the lives of the students we teach and transform school culture far beyond the walls of our classroom.

We as teachers make a significant impact on the lives of the students we teach, and our inspiration can create a passion for education and a respect for humanity in students. Take teaching to the next level by being more than a teacher, by becoming the mentor they need, and by taking on a role more powerful than who just reads off facts on a page.

Educators can help our students to work harder, to value their education, to overcome something traumatic, or even to be more mindful of what they can be thankful for. Teachers can help students learn to say, "I love you, Mom." We can remind them of what their families do for them and to be appreciative of that. Often we have to be the voice of reason or persuasion for them, and we need to all be in this together, so have those conversations and challenge colleagues to do the same.

Getting to the Next Level

Using our platforms for more than academics is one of the best things we can do to create a positive culture in our schools while helping our students learn life lessons and aiding them to become better people. We have to look at ourselves and understand there is a much more important mission than passing a state test at the end of the school year. We have to take our students to the next level, to teach more than facts on a page, and to be a voice and support for the students who have none. Find the right moments to give them hope. If we are real with our students, they will better connect with what we are trying to teach them. So be that teacher!

Takeaways

- Tell your story and don't shy away from using your moments of struggle or failure as powerful lessons.
- Conversations about life are opportunities we as educators must take hold of and use to positively influence the culture of our classrooms and schools.
- Challenge other educators to teach not only content but life lessons.

Chapter Nine

It's the Little Things

By now you know that I have always strived to outwork anyone in the room. This was true even in my middle school basketball days. When I was the smallest student in the entire school, I could still cut through the defense and score almost at will. One game I dropped twenty points. After the final buzzer I thought my dad was going to go wild and say, "I can't believe you scored twenty points!"

Instead, he taught me one of the most valuable lessons of my life.

He said, "Son, you can score anytime you want. Now you need to get everyone else involved. You have to build the team up by giving them a chance."

Soon my goal was to get a double-double in every game. That meant I aimed to score double-digit points, but more importantly, I would get at least ten assists by passing the ball to my teammates to score.

I've never forgotten those words. They formed my idea of what it means to take teaching to the next level: you need to get everyone else involved.

If you only focus on you and your classroom, you only make yourself and your own classroom better. Once your classroom is where it needs to be, your job is to build the team. To make the team better, build the school culture and get involved anywhere you can.

Aiming for the Double-Double

A school cannot operate efficiently without teachers being actively involved in doing the little things.

Years ago, I was an assistant coach to my wife, Jaime, who was a great collegiate athlete. Together we ran a JV girls basketball program at the high school level. The first day of open gym, our team knew absolutely nothing about basketball, and my wife and I discussed how much we needed to teach them. One of our players was asked to play a post position close to the hoop because she was tall. When asked to post up—which means to stand in position with the defender against your back, ready to get the ball and score—the young girl, who would go on to become one of our best players, said, "What, you mean stand like a pencil?" My wife and I said to each other, "This is going to be a long season."

Our players worked harder than we could have expected, and we went on to be a very successful team with a great record, but that didn't happen overnight. It took a lot of practice and most of all, it took every player understanding they had an important role. They had to know that to win they must execute even the smallest details to the best of their ability. They were diligently coached to understand that winning in basketball requires much more than each player worrying solely about herself or trying to score the most points. Every player needs to perform their role on the court to perfection. They need to understand where to be at all times, and they must do the little things. Our team understood that it was the little things, like boxing out and getting the rebound on a missed shot, setting perfect screens against the defense so shooters can get open, or diving for loose balls on the floor, that would allow them to outhustle and defeat much "better" teams. For the team to be successful, it cannot be all about shooting and scoring the most points. Those things are what everyone sees, but they're not what wins games.

The most successful teams in sports, regardless of the sport, do the little things with finesse. These things may seem unimportant; they are not as flashy as scoring a touchdown, hitting a home run, or shooting the winning shot. No, most often the operational tactics go unseen, yet if they are not done, the game cannot be won. Sure, a touchdown might end up on a highlight reel, but it is the offensive lineman making a big block that enabled the quarterback to make that touchdown throw. It is the countless hours of practice hitting off a tee that yields the perfect swing that becomes a home run in the bottom of the ninth inning. It is the basketball player who sets the perfect screen that allows the shooter to get open and hit the game-winning shot.

Can you honestly say you did your very best today to move your school in the right direction?

It's the little things that pay dividends and separate average teams from championship teams. They may seem like small, insignificant aspects of sports, yet if you ask any Hall of Fame coach, they will tell you that a team cannot win without them. Vince Lombardi, the legendary coach of the Green Bay Packers, said, "Winning means you are willing to go longer, work harder, and give more than anyone else." Doing things that are not flashy, that go unseen, and do not get your name in the paper might be the difference between success or failure.

The same ideas hold true as they relate to teachers and their influence on their classrooms and school environments. Teachers doing the little things can make or break a school. A lively school environment has many moving parts. The big aspects like student engagement, behavior management, and student-teacher relationships play perhaps the most important role in cultural change. But it's the little things educators do every day that allow those big forces to make their impact.

Get involved in after-school events; hype up the crowd at football or basketball games; make an impression around the school, in the hallways, or at lunch. Walk the halls during your planning period just to check passes and high-five students. Take time to check in on classes with substitute teachers, supporting both the teacher and the administration while making sure students are focused on their work. Be in the stands at football games getting the students to start the wave or a strong, spirited school chant. Attend their concert and be the teacher they look for in the crowd of a few hundred people. Ask a table of students to invite the student sitting alone to join them or establish an opportunity for students to take leadership roles. Educational game changers Darrin Peppard and Bradlee Skinner facilitated a program where student leaders served coffee and doughnuts to parents and bus drivers at the start of the school day, showing their appreciation and enriching the bond between school and community.

Eye of the Storm

Doing the little things is not a September and October thing. It is not a Monday and Tuesday thing. It is an everyday, all-year thing, and it is not just for the classroom teacher but every educator who walks the halls in the building. What you do in August you better be doing in May!

Routines are key. You cannot lead an effective classroom, or school for that matter, in chaos. The same goes for inciting great cultural change. There has to be an element of order for you to build off of with tools like energy, excitement, and entertainment.

Establishing order and structure in a classroom creates calm. My students are seventh grade "adults"—at least they think they are. I love teaching this age group. I care about them and their success, which they will only realize later in life. Many are fortunate to have supportive families, but for many the only structure they see is within the walls of the school building. They come from a variety of backgrounds. Some have faced immigration, abuse, split families; others have been raised by grandparents or have parents who are always working and never home; some are even faced with the responsibility of raising their own siblings. My classroom needs to be a sanctuary for all of them.

In order to establish a classroom culture of order, I keep steady routines. Each day in the early weeks I go over my expectations. The more students hear those expectations, the more they see what happens when they're met, the more they hold each other accountable for them. When you walk into my classroom in September, you will see students raising their hands to ask to sharpen their pencils, and you'll see the same thing in May and June. By establishing what students should expect—even for simple acts like sharpening pencils—and sticking to them, I create a place where all students feel safe and calm.

Can we expect students who don't feel safe to grow academically?

Out and About

There are no shadows in education, you cannot stand off to the side and expect good things to happen. Often, fellow educator Thomas Annunziata and I take time during our free periods to walk the halls of the school, from one end to the other and down every hallway. Part of why we do this is to check student passes and find students skipping classes, and we even check in on classes with substitute teachers. This supports schoolwide initiatives but also supports our fellow educators. But the most important aspect of it is that we are seen in every corner of the school, walking by every classroom and having positive interactions, smiling, and high-fiving students.

One of the strongest ways to move your school forward and make your presence known is during moments where you are supervising students outside your classroom. Small moments are where the little things make profound impacts. Do you take those opportunities to sit down and take time off? Or are you capitalizing on the small moments during the day to make your school better?

Your school culture will not move in the right direction unless teachers and educators use every opportunity to make the school better. Some lessons are best taught outside of the classroom. Lunch duty, assemblies, and hallway interactions, although seemingly unimportant, are times when you can set expectations for how students act outside of the classroom and empower those who need a voice. Students will learn how to interact with each other and adults.

There is so much to gain from moments during the school day that so many teachers never see. Too few of them are even looking for those moments. I do not waste a single opportunity—honestly, to the point where it sometimes wears me out. But I'm willing to take that chance, because what evolves from those opportunities can have a lasting impact. You have to take action as often as possible.

When others may try to find moments to sit down or check out, move around and get involved with students. Have a quick chat with a student in the hallway. Give a kind smile that shows you see them. It might be brief and seem unimportant. But the next time you see that student being disruptive at an assembly and you lock eyes, they might just change their behavior immediately because during that brief conversation a mutual respect was built and a relationship began to develop. They might not be a student in our classroom, but all students are our students.

On the Lookout

People are the most important asset in a school. Good people create a welcoming environment where students feel happy and therefore work harder. You cannot buy this; no laptop cart or trendy strategy can match an effective educator. No fashionable program can affect academic growth as much as a positive environment generated by teachers who set routines and have high expectations. In part, that's because none of those things have heart. They can't respond to student's emotional needs and find opportunities to connect with kids.

As often as I can, I look for the one student who seems to be alone, the kid who might be seated next to other students but has no friends or is considered uncool by others. I make it my personal mission to sit with them and get them laughing and involved. I find ways to pull others into the conversation or get the group of students around them laughing. Sometimes if I have a good relationship with a student sitting nearby, I'll get them to ask the student to join their group. Changing the day for one student and teaching students about caring for other people is a two-for-one deal.

Next-level teaching is all about finding ways to connect with students. It's one of the most powerful things I do. Every day I try to pick at least one student to connect with in my class and one student who is not in my class. I look for anything to start a conversation—little things they say or the shirt they're wearing—that will bridge the gap and begin the formation of a positive relationship. Each day after that I say hello or fist bump and smile at them. Your smile may be the only smile they see all day. Those two little power plays can be game changers. You never know how that one interaction, even just a smile, will change the day of a student.

Each interaction has the potential to snowball. A teacher who cares can change the outcome of one student's experience in the hallway. The rest of that student's day will be different. That student will move through the rest of their school day with a new mentality and have more positive interactions with peers in the building. Those peers will have more positive interactions with students and adults as the day goes along. One fist bump will have affected the whole school.

Now imagine what happens when interactions like that happen not just with one student but with your entire class and then with every student you encounter in the school, not just once a day, but all day, every day of the school year. You can incite a monumental shift in school culture with just a minimal amount of effort. Something so little, but so contagious.

We focus so much on building positive relationships with students, but what about parents? According to elementary school principal Deborah Ellis:

> It's so important to not take small things for granted because small things pay off in big ways! I've even surprised students by showing up at their bus stop in the morning. Those extra minutes of connecting with the kids provide that extra attention that students sometimes need. In addition to positive phone calls home, teachers should be encouraged to make home visits, go to those weekend soccer games, and attend those church baptisms even though they are after "contract hours." Through these continued positive interactions, families begin to not only see you as their child's teacher, you become a part of their family.

In building those parent partnerships, we also forge a community of support. A positive phone call to a parent can demonstrate the level of caring and support you have for a child, and it allows for student-teacher relationships to grow. Early in the year I try to make two positive phone calls home a week. A positive conversation with a parent changes how that parent will interact with you in the future, but it also changes how the student will act in your classroom for the rest of the school year. It will turn a bad attitude into a "yes, sir," and it will turn a lack of effort into a "wow, this is the best project I have seen all year."

Be a teacher who sees things in a positive light rather than being negative. Get involved in after-school events and small school activities. Ramp up spirit week. Be the driving force of the canned-food drive. Challenge other classes to outdo your own in raising money for cancer research. Walk the halls with purpose looking to address behavior but also to interact with students. Become a coach, start an after-school club, or get involved in tutoring. Doing the little things is making sure you're present all the time and taking it upon yourself to get students excited about things they normally would not care about. Be that teacher your school needs, and do not stand on the sidelines of your school. Go where the game is played by getting involved and taking action.

Can you honestly say you did your very best today to move your school in the right direction? That's the powerful question we must ask ourselves every day.

Looking in the Mirror

But what about the educators? Are we following the same guidelines we set for our students? Or are we setting rules and expectations for our students that we ourselves will not follow. Are we listening during school meetings, sure to be on time, and working as hard as we can each day? How can we ask students to do things that we as educators and professionals are not doing?

We spend so much time building relationships with students, but what about the people around us? Doing the little things also means treating other teachers in the building with respect. Students learn how to speak and interact with their peers and other adults by watching their teachers. So, help out when a substitute teacher is in the building. Go and pop your head in the classroom just to say hello, letting the students know to be on their best behavior. Building relationships with fellow teachers is just as much a teaching tool as a great lesson plan. You have become a role model; when you do not think students are watching, they are. Those interactions can mold their behavior with other teachers, peers, and adults in their life. A powerful change can only be created by something small like seeing one teacher smile at another in the hallway or supporting another teacher in a time of need.

Many educators come to our school to see how a once-failing school like ours was able to become accredited in just one year after we welcomed Hamish Brewer, perhaps the most famous principal on the planet, to our ranks. The relentless skateboarding tattooed principal turned our school around from the depths of failure to a new future of prosperity with great policies and the establishment of an environment of love and support for students and staff. That turnaround, as successful as it has been, will only continue to be as effective as the educators willing to do whatever it takes to capture the moment and continue the work to make it happen. I do not believe perfect teachers exist. But at our school, there are many teachers and educators who go beyond the call of duty and look for every opportunity to make a difference in a student's life.

Message from an Educational Leader

Physical education teacher Jordan Fisher, one of the educational leaders at his elementary school in northern Virginia, exemplifies a teacher who does the little things each day. Here, he speaks to the importance of how the little things can change both the classroom and school culture and looking at everything as an opportunity to make a positive change.

There is a difference between schools that are successful, schools that have high student and staff engagement, few student behavioral issues, high achievement and test scores etc., and schools that are unsuccessful, which have a deficit in those areas. Successful schools have teachers and staff who have completely bought in and are willing to do the little things to ensure that their students succeed. They are building a school environment where you will see full potential reached in all areas.

It's true that one of the best things you can do for your students is to make your class exciting. Make it a class they look forward to going to and be *that* teacher for them. But what does not get talked about, what gets thrown to the wayside because we put so much time and effort into developing those Pinterest-worthy lesson plans or getting our students to pass those standardized tests, is taking the time out of your day to do the little things, to be fully bought in and invested in turning around your school's environment, both in terms of academics and behavior.

These little things are required not just in your classroom but throughout the building, not just with your students but with every student within those walls. These little things actually become the big reasons why schools are successful or are not. We could discuss for chapters what these little things are, but I'll just name a few: going out of your way for little day-to-day interactions with students, making a big deal out of school events, going to clubs after school to have fun with students, or having a presence in the hallways—before class begins, after class ends, and during transitions, lunches, your lunch, or your planning period. Ensure students are quiet and respectful during assemblies. Do not ignore behavioral issues you see in the hall or pretend you did not see them because you would rather not deal with them. Bring passion to all you do. Go all out on school dress-up days or spirit days. Familiarize yourself with what is popular among your students (e.g., video games, movies, songs, dances, sports teams). Check in on students who seem down and know when they seem off or are not themselves. Create special handshakes with students. Ask open-ended questions to get them talking and not giving you just yes or no answers. We could go on and on.

Students notice. Students will follow your lead. And you will see their willingness to do things for you, the school, and their peers increase. Doing the little things is what makes or breaks your school environment. Honestly, this should be something that comes naturally to us; it's the reason we got into teaching in the first place: to care for students who do not feel cared about and making learning fun. So, it should not be hard for us. Can you, in good conscience, say you did your best each day to make sure students felt loved, included, safe? That you helped them enjoy your class and follow the rules? This is the most important question you need to be asking. This is the question that will make or break your school environment. This is next-level teaching. Doing the little things is easy. You need to be all in for your students and your school.

Getting to the Next Level

Creating great cultural change in your classroom and school extends far beyond the lesson plan and far beyond the reach of your principal. Everyone plays a role; a school cannot move forward without the correct pieces in place. But teachers are the driving force and at the heart of any positive change. Schools cannot improve without the buy-in and consistent effort of great teachers willing to go to the next level not only for the students, but for each other. Because teachers make a tremendous impact not only on the lives of their students, but on each other! When another teacher sees what you are doing and notices you doing the "little things," they will follow your lead. Even the most introverted teachers can make profound impacts on their schools by setting an example.

Making your school better involves everyone working as a team and doing the little things every day. Set expectations and be a positive role model by meeting them. Take time to walk the halls and have upbeat interactions with students. Look to build relationships with every student, and teach students to build each other up.

These aspects of education do not get talked about enough, but they are the gasoline that moves the machine. They fuel the school's drive forward and allow academic and behavioral growth of students. The implications will be seen in the culture of the building with smiling teachers and smiling students all working together to accomplish the same goals. Next-level teachers work as a team to support student academic success, positive behavior, and great school environment.

Takeaways

- The little things can make or break a school's culture.
- Be out and about, and be an active member of the school.
- Students will follow your lead, so practice what you preach!

Next-Level Discussion

Think about your school culture. What are some of the "little things" that could use more attention in your school or classroom?

Conclusion

Always Be
That Teacher

*M*y wife, one of the best and most genuine educators I have ever known, once asked, "If you're not in this to make lasting impressions on their lives, why are you in it?"

One thing I wish my college education prepared me for was that teaching is not about facts, numbers, equations, or staff meetings. Teaching is not really about educating students on state standards. Teaching is about preparing students, young and old, to face a harsh and unfeeling world with the confidence that they are truly ready to conquer life. Teaching is about instilling a fire in our students to achieve and to never hold back. It is giving our students a place to be themselves and the comfort of constancy in a world of change. Teaching is about being so on fire for your students that they will remember the times when you stood on tables, dressed up in costumes, and had them laughing and crying at the same time. In these moments, it is not about memorizing facts, it is about creating an atmosphere of love, trust, and—most of all—*fun.*

To be successful at anything you have to know why you are doing it. For educators, knowing your purpose could be the important force that gets you through long nights of grading and the worst of days. Purpose is what gets us to get up every day. It allows us to be excited and to create a positive change in our schools even when we are exhausted and feel overworked. It is what creates that passion and that fire in your soul. It is what moves you on a personal level to take on one of the most difficult and demanding jobs you can choose. It's the one thing that you have to remember because for you, it makes this more than a job.

If you're not in this to make *lasting impressions* on their lives, why are you in it?

For me, my purpose is to be *that* teacher for my students. No matter if you loved school or hated school, we all had that teacher that we still remember, the teacher that did it for us, the one that changed what education meant and looked like. It might have been the teacher who jumped on top of tables or the one that made you laugh. It might have been an incredible academic experience, or it might have been a teacher who simply gave you the time of day when others walked past you. It might have been the teacher that did more than teach content and made the school day different for you in a way that no other teacher did.

We may not be able to remember much about school, but we remember *that* teacher. This is my purpose: to be the one person my students will remember the rest of their lives. Years down the long road of their lives, I want my class to be the class that comes up in conversations. I unapologetically go beyond for my students, and I hold nothing back. I don't always know the life my student has walking into my classroom, but I know the life they will have while they are in it. I want to create the lasting change that they need and that every student deserves.

In order to be the best for our students we need to move away from negativity and become providers of solutions. In this day and age, many people have used social media to make a positive impact in the world and inspire action. But there is also the flip side where people have become phenomenal keyboard warriors, sending out messages about what the world should look like, what life should be like, and how schools should operate. Far too often those people are not doing anything to make change but are comfortable on the sidelines telling others what they should be doing.

In life, in education, in your profession, you have to put yourself out there and forget the fear of failure. When you are creating something special for your students and your school, forget about the worry that it might not work out. When you live with those worries, you live in a world of limitations, constrained by self-doubt and the fear of putting yourself out there and trying something new. Do not fall into the trap of talking about the problems in education, your school, or your leadership. Be part of the solution. Be better for your students. That is what will make them remember you. Do something special. If you fail, at least it was doing something more than filling the air with words of negativity. You were the teacher that stood up, took a stand, and took a swing at bringing about some real change. You do not live in a world of words, but a world of actions.

I have found that people often believe there are limits to what can be done and what our schools' potential and the outcomes of our classrooms can be. We teach our students to fly high and shoot for the stars, but many of us have a very different perspective.

If teaching were easy, *everyone would do it.*

Our schools and our students deserve the very best from us. Do we fill the halls with negativity, complaining about what our school doesn't have or how everything could be done better? Or do we find solutions to the problems that plague our schools? Are we comfortable with the school we have, or are we willing to step up and dream of something a little better for our students? The success of your teaching, your classroom, and your school rests on your ability to look outside the box and never settle for an average result.

Being a next-level teacher means you are not OK with an average school or classroom and you are not afraid to fail. When it comes to attempting to win over a student, I may fail nine out of ten times. It is that one out of ten that makes all the difference. That is what makes teaching so inspiring. You continue to fight for a student's future and win a student over who has been told they never had a chance.

Fighting for the students' futures was left off the job description because it is so difficult, but it is one of the most important parts of what we do. If teaching were easy, everyone would do it. But teaching is far from easy, it is one of the most difficult jobs in the world. Even the best teachers, like the best athletes, hit a slump. The year is long and challenging. There is no off button for people involved in education. Teachers cannot just shut down when they are having a bad day or are overtired or have sick children at home. You have to bring your best every single day, and sometimes you have to remind yourself just how important you are to the lives of those who look up at you each day.

I remember my wife and I discussing our daughter's first days of kindergarten. We agreed that more than anything else, we wanted our daughter to learn to love school. To us the most important thing was that she enjoyed every day and loved her teacher, Ms. Richmond. We wanted our daughter to be excited to see her teacher every single morning. And that's what happened. She would wake up every day ready to go, and the learning would take flight. That is why we do what we do; it is not an obligation to standards, numbers, and obscure facts. This job is not about data meetings, lesson-plan templates, professional learning communities, or collaborative learning teams. It is the most demanding job on the planet created for the strongest of us to continue the grind of building children up, making them feel valued, and teaching them about hard work. We provide a path for their success.

To be that teacher, ask yourself a hard question: "Would I want my child to be in my class?" To be a teacher your students will remember, you have to make every day count and hold nothing back. Everyone wants to know the number one magical trick to making their class the best in the school. Likewise, everyone wants to know the trick to turn around a failing school. From my experience, working at a middle school that went from failing to succeeding, I can tell you it was the total uprooting of a negative and deteriorating culture to make room for something different. We created something that excited the students. Every day and any day could bring something new. This has to be the mission of all educators. We need to bring about change, but it's got to be the right kind of change: rooted in love for our students and our unmatched desire to become the teacher that our students will always remember.

Next-Level Teaching Doesn't Just Change the Life of a Child. It Changes Entire Families.

I want to share a powerful letter I received from a parent:

> As a parent of two children who suffer from a neurological disorder that causes physical delays and sensory processing issues, I appreciate just how important it is for a teacher to love my kids. I have had entire school semesters where I can count the number of good days that my kids had at school on one hand. My kids struggle to attract friends and communicate with their peers. They are keenly aware of how different they are and very sensitive to others noticing it. They act out and can't always tell you why. They lash out when what they really want is a hug. My kids are the ones that make a teacher's life more difficult every day.
>
> My kids do not thrive in a normal classroom environment. They don't thrive in the normal gym or music class. But they can still thrive. I have seen it. I've seen teachers notice what no one else could. Teachers who are willing to take on some of their pain and not just respond to their behavior. Teachers who step in at just the right moment can turn an entire day around. Those moments may have seemed so small, but they have changed the lives of everyone in my entire family.
>
> I want every teacher that my kids have for the rest of their lives to read this book. I want them re-energized and reminded of what

is really important: that kids who are loved are much more likely to succeed. That kids like mine can far surpass expectations. That they have a beautiful and meaningful responsibility in kids' lives. I want them to be reminded that next-level teaching doesn't just change the life of a child. It changes the lives of entire families.

Jeremy Porter,

Parent

We are all writing the story of our lives. What is the ending of yours going to look like? When people learn your story what will they think? What will they take away from it? What will they think you did with your life? Dare to dream that you can create the most amazing classroom and school experience for your students, because dreams can become a reality through our actions. We have to take hold of our present and create a better future.

The truest fact in teaching is this: students need you! Next-level teaching is about so much more than facts on a page or data. At the end of the day, even if your lesson plan didn't go so great, were *you* great for students? Be *that* teacher *that* day for students. Walk by and smile, acknowledge them, and let them know that you see them. Students just want to feel part of the game. As next-level teachers, we have more than the opportunity to put them into the game; we have the power to make them feel like they are the game. In your class, they can be the most important person on the planet.

If you want to be that teacher for your students, you have to think like your back is against a wall and you are determined to face the challenges of making your classroom and school the best it can be. The wall is your best friend because when your back is against it, you have nowhere else to run but forward.

Dare to dream, and make the ending to your story something worth telling. Create it from the passion and desire to accomplish and cultivate a classroom culture that others desperately want to be a part of. The effects of what you build will flow from your door throughout the halls of your school. Dare to dream and the river of your passion will rush through every classroom and flood the future of every student with something truly special.

Take your teaching to the next level, and establish a culture that is unmatched, built on excitement and engagement, and so much fun that it becomes a powerful force that washes over everything you touch! What are you going to do to become *that* teacher? Walk with a heart fueled with passion to make an impact on the lives of educators and students alike. Our job is the hardest job in the world, and it takes guts to step up. But anything worth doing is tough—and we rise together! Game-changing is not a cliché; it is a way of life. Some talk about it while others live by it.

Invite Jonathan Alsheimer to your next professional development event!

Speaking Topics

Next-Level Teaching

Keynote session for educational conferences, professional development, and staff development. "Next-Level Teaching" shows how every teacher can bring their unique flair to better their classroom and school every single day. Too often teachers believe that culture and climate stop at the threshold of their principal's door; however, teachers have an incredible influence and ability to create a wave of positive impact on the outcomes of both the classroom and school environment.

Go to the next level, engage your students, establish community partnerships, build powerful relationships, and create a contagious classroom and school atmosphere!

That Teacher

Keynote session for educational conferences, professional development, and staff development. "That Teacher" is an inspiring message where Jonathan Alsheimer reminds educators about their why in education. He advises teachers to "die with memories, not dreams" and not to look back wondering what they could have accomplished. Reclaim the motivation that created a passionate desire to make an impact on the world. No matter if you loved school or hated school, you always remember *that teacher* who made a difference in your life. In this session, Jonathan Alsheimer motivates educators to reignite that flame to be *that teacher* that they needed when they were younger.

Next-Level Leaders: Insights from a Next-Level Teacher

Keynote session for leaders and administrators at education conferences, leadership professional development events, and leadership retreats.

These are the lessons from a next-level teacher and how a leader can get their teachers to transform the culture of their school to bring energy, engagement, and rigor into the classroom.

Every leader has the potential to be as influential in students' lives as the teacher. Jonathan will bring this to life and refuel your leaders to step back into the school ready to lead to the next level.

Next-Level Impact

Student session for student assembly audiences. "Next-Level Impact" is about how students can make a greater impact on their schools, their peers, and their lives through maximum effort, building relationships, overcoming adversity, and focusing on their influence.

Students will be motivated and inspired to take their education and their life to new heights. A message aimed to motivate students to work harder, to take care of one another and their teachers, to get involved in their schools, and to look for ways to make a positive impact on the people around them.

Don't just talk about change; show them how to become leaders!

Acknowledgments

I would like to thank all the amazing teachers and leaders in education with whom I have been so privileged to serve with. We have the most important job on the planet: leading and inspiring students to pursue their dreams with passion. Thank you to those who have supported me over the years and, most of all, to those who have provided continued support for this book.

Thank you to Hamish Brewer for being a major part of *Next-Level Teaching* and writing an amazing foreword. Being on this journey and creating a wave of change in education with you has been a true honor.

To my brother Daniel Alsheimer, illustrator and artistic mastermind of the book's incredible cover, thank you, not only for being a part of my book and being family but also for being a friend and having my back. Visit www.DanielAlsheimer.com to connect with Daniel Alsheimer and work with him.

Finally, I would like to thank my family. Thank you to my mom, Kimrae Alsheimer, and my father, John Alsheimer. You raised me to be true to myself, to work hard, and to leave it all on the field. I believe that I do that in this book and that I live it every day. Thank you, Dad, for being an inspiration in the classroom and in life. Mom, thank you for your strength through your continued struggle with cancer. Your truest self came out in those moments of pain and struggle, and you are pure at heart and selfless. I love you both.

Most of all thank you to my beautiful wife, Jaime Leigh Alsheimer. Your unmatched love and continued inspiration provided me with the drive to spill my passion out on paper. You motivate me to be the hardest worker in the room. You make me a better person, and for that I love you with all of my heart. My girls, Adleigh Noelle, Sadie Quinn, and my wife, are my motivation. I love you with everything I have.

About the Author

*J*onathan Alsheimer is the unorthodox, energetic, and entertaining middle school teacher who refuses to live a life of limitations and works with UFC fighters, celebrities, and clothing brands to take his classroom and school to the next level.

A husband, a father of two beautiful daughters, a passionate educator, a Teacher of the Year, and a national keynote speaker, Jonathan Alsheimer believes teachers are the driving force of lively classrooms and school culture. In addition to being an educator, Jonathan Alsheimer also travels and speaks to student assemblies about overcoming adversity, giving maximum effort, respecting others, and striving to make an impact on schools in a session entitled "Next-Level Impact."

Jonathan teaches at the world-renowned Fred Lynn Middle School, which was featured in two documentaries, *Relentless* and *Relentless: Chasing Accreditation.* He was featured as the teacher who forged a partnership with UFC fighter and lightweight contender Paul Felder to send messages about never giving up, fighting for education, and empowering students to believe in themselves, all principles that Jonathan promotes in his classroom.

Jonathan also partnered with Fear the Fighter, an MMA clothing brand, to establish an antibullying campaign with "Relentless" Principal Hamish Brewer.

Jonathan didn't stop there. He formed a partnership with Chris "Drama" Pfaff, an MTV reality star and CEO of Young and Reckless, to bring clothing to his students in need and to build student leadership in his school.

As Jonathan always says, "Game-changing is not a cliché; it is a way of life. Some talk about it while others live by it."

More from

DAVE BURGESS
Consulting, inc.

$\mathcal{S}$ince 2012, DBCI has been publishing books that inspire and equip educators to be their best. For more information on our titles or to purchase bulk orders for your school, district, or book study, visit DaveBurgessconsulting.com/DBCIbooks.

More Leadership & School Culture

Culturize by Jimmy Casas
Escaping the School Leader's Dunk Tank by Rebecca Coda and Rick Jetter
From Teacher to Leader by Starr Sackstein
The Innovator's Mind-set by George Couros
Kids Deserve It! by Todd Nesloney and Adam Welcome
Let Them Speak by Rebecca Coda and Rick Jetter
The Limitless School by Abe Hege and Adam Dovico
The Pepper Effect by Sean Gaillard
The Principled Principal by Jeffrey Zoul and Anthony McConnell
Relentless by Hamish Brewer
The Secret Solution by Todd Whitaker, Sam Miller, and Ryan Donlan
Start. Right. Now. by Todd Whitaker, Jeffrey Zoul, and Jimmy Casas
Stop. Right. Now. by Jimmy Casas and Jeffrey Zoul
They Call Me "Mr. De" by Frank DeAngelis
Unmapped Potential by Julie Hasson and Missy Lennard
Word Shift by Joy Kirr
Your School Rocks by Ryan McLane and Eric Lowe

Like a PIRATE™ Series

Teach Like a PIRATE by Dave Burgess
eXPlore Like a Pirate by Michael Matera
Learn Like a Pirate by Paul Solarz
Play Like a Pirate by Quinn Rollins
Run Like a Pirate by Adam Welcome

Lead Like a PIRATE™ Series

Lead Like a PIRATE by Shelley Burgess and Beth Houf
Balance Like a Pirate by Jessica Cabeen, Jessica Johnson, and Sarah Johnson
Lead beyond Your Title by Nili Bartley
Lead with Culture by Jay Billy
Lead with Literacy by Mandy Ellis

Technology & Tools

50 Things You Can Do with Google Classroom by Alice Keeler and Libbi Miller
50 Things to Go Further with Google Classroom by Alice Keeler and Libbi Miller
140 Twitter Tips for Educators by Brad Currie, Billy Krakower, and Scott Rocco
Block Breaker by Brian Aspinall
Code Breaker by Brian Aspinall
Google Apps for Littles by Christine Pinto and Alice Keeler
Master the Media by Julie Smith
Shake Up Learning by Kasey Bell
Social LEADia by Jennifer Casa-Todd
Teaching Math with Google Apps by Alice Keeler and Diana Herrington
Teachingland by Amanda Fox and Mary Ellen Weeks

Teaching Methods & Materials

All 4s and 5s by Andrew Sharos
The Classroom Chef by John Stevens and Matt Vaudrey
Ditch That Homework by Matt Miller and Alice Keeler
Ditch That Textbook by Matt Miller
Don't Ditch That Tech by Matt Miller, Nate Ridgway, and Angelia Ridgway
EDrenaline Rush by John Meehan
Educated by Design by Michael Cohen, The Tech Rabbi
The EduProtocol Field Guide by Marlena Hebern and Jon Corippo
The EduProtocol Field Guide: Book 2 by Marlena Hebern and Jon Corippo
Instant Relevance by Denis Sheeran
LAUNCH by John Spencer and A. J. Juliani
Make Learning MAGICAL by Tisha Richmond
Pure Genius by Don Wettrick
The Revolution by Darren Ellwein and Derek McCoy
Shift This! by Joy Kirr
Spark Learning by Ramsey Musallam
Sparks in the Dark by Travis Crowder and Todd Nesloney
Table Talk Math by John Stevens
The Wild Card by Hope and Wade King
The Writing on the Classroom Wall by Steve Wyborney

Inspiration, Professional Growth & Personal Development

Be REAL by Tara Martin
Be the One for Kids by Ryan Sheehy
Creatively Productive by Lisa Johnson
The EduNinja Mind-set by Jennifer Burdis
Empower Our Girls by Lynmara Colón and Adam Welcome
The Four O'Clock Faculty by Rich Czyz
How Much Water Do We Have? by Pete and Kris Nunweiler
P Is for Pirate by Dave and Shelley Burgess
A Passion for Kindness by Tamara Letter

The Path to Serendipity by Allyson Apsey
Sanctuaries by Dan Tricarico
Shattering the Perfect Teacher Myth by Aaron Hogan
Stories from Webb by Todd Nesloney
Talk to Me by Kim Bearden
Teach Me, Teacher by Jacob Chastain
TeamMakers by Laura Robb and Evan Robb
Through the Lens of Serendipity by Allyson Apsey
The Zen Teacher by Dan Tricarico

Children's Books

Beyond Us by Aaron Polansky
Cannonball In by Tara Martin
Dolphins in Trees by Aaron Polansky
I Want to Be a Lot by Ashley Savage
The Princes of Serendip by Allyson Apsey
Zom-Be a Design Thinker by Amanda Fox